All colour book of Biblical Myths & Mysteries

Gilbert Thurlow

Photographs by
Sonia Halliday

Octopus Books

БѢГСТВО ІИССОВО ВО ЕГѴПЕ

Contents

EDITED BY BRIDGET HADAWAY

First published 1974
by Octopus Books Limited
a division of the Octopus Publishing Group
Michelin House, 81 Fulham Road,
London SW3 6RB

© 1974 Octopus Books Limited
Reprinted 1989

ISBN 0 7064 5067 1

Produced by Mandarin Offset
Printed in Hong Kong

Introduction

What is a myth? In its narrowest sense it is a tale about the supernatural. But in a deeper sense it is also a revelation of the divine in terms of this life, a method of revealing ultimate truth. In this book we are using the word in its technical sense of describing other-worldly matters in this-worldly concepts. We are using the Old and New Testaments of the Bible to trace the growth of the consciousness of man and of the divine life in him. The theme of man's origin and nature as pursued in the first book of the Old Testament has much in common with the literature of Babylon, Canaan, Egypt, and with folk-lore in many other lands around the world. Babylonian and Egyptian civilizations depended on agriculture. This in turn depended on the behaviour of their rivers, and it was believed that the rivers could be controlled by ritual activities evoking supernatural phenomena. These activities, repeated annually, largely revolved around the New Year festivities, conducted by the king and concerned with the victory of a divine force over chaos. The Hebrew people took such myths and mysteries into their national traditions.

But the Hebrews performed a function of unique value in raising the ultimate purpose of divine worship from a prayer for successful agriculture to a right relationship with God. From its first verse, the Bible treats the early myths in the context of 'God above us' whilst the myths of other religions are 'built up from below'. They treat of gods and people and phenomena of the world around and beneath us – and once we have climbed Olympus, it is equally beneath us. Greek gods and heroes interact amongst each other, but, although biblical language contains many relics of such conceptions – such as God walking in the Garden of Eden – Genesis was compiled long after the Jews had progressed to the conception of God as one, compared with whom all other 'gods' were as nothing. Further, the divine figures of Greece and Rome and Egypt were amoral. The goodness or badness of their actions was reckoned as less important than the convenience or inconvenience of their results. But God in the Bible, from its very first chapter, is seen as 'good'. Man is to obey God's good will and disobedience brings dire consequences.

The early narratives in the Bible conform to the historical definition of myth, in that Adam, Eve, Cain, Abel, Noah, and others named in them are not to be seen as individuals who lived in certain times and places. They are instead, far more important and relevant to us as timeless types of human nature who constantly recur. Man and woman, Adam and Eve, each possess a dual nature. They are 'created in the image of God', that is, their true nature and destiny are the eternal sharing in the beauty, truth and goodness which are everlasting, while at the same time they are also in a body which is of dust and must return to dust. As a result, they are constantly in a state of tension, and drive themselves further away from their creator by disobedience to divine wisdom.

The next theme after creation, that of the human tragedy, is again paralleled in myths of many peoples. It includes the serpent bringing both knowledge and deception, man's rebellion, the expulsion from paradise, the loss of immortality, and thereafter the necessity for painful childbearing and work.

The compiler of Genesis saw that there were two kinds of knowledge, the first being the realization that obedience to the holy God is essential for man's relationship with Him. But there was, secondly, the knowledge forbidden to man. In the myths he used, this was the knowledge of the power of spells and ritual activities by which nature's forces could be controlled. Misuse of such spells was held to have led man to forfeit immortality. In such myths a Serpent appears in various guises. He brings wisdom ('Be wise as serpents' Matt. 10;16) and healing (cf., the brazen serpent erected by Moses in the wilderness), but in Genesis the serpent is the deceiver, luring man to death. In related myths the serpent steals the fruit of immortality from man, robbing him of it, and keeping it for himself, so that instead of dying he merely casts his skin. Christian art from the third century onwards shows Adam and Eve standing either side of the tree, round which the serpent is coiled; sometimes she takes the fruit from the serpent's mouth, sometimes from the tree itself. By the mediaeval period the fruit has become an apple, though neither in the Bible nor in early tradition was this so.

So the free and happy relationship between man and God is broken. He is driven out of Eden. Henceforth there is the long warfare between good and evil. Sex has become a thing of shame, childbearing a painful struggle, agriculture a weary toil; while cherubim bar the way to the tree of life.

Time passes. In a world whose population is growing, different types of community come into being. The Cain and Abel myth personifies these, the one tills the soil, the other is a shepherd. Abel's ritual is successful, Cain's is not; he has not performed his ritual properly. The myth behind the murder of Abel may recall a ritual slaying intended to fertilize the soil. Cain flees, yet is protected by God. Babylonian practices suggest that he has become defiled by his ritual, yet is sacred for he has secured fertility for the soil, and when purified he may return home. The myth also provides an explanation of the age-long feud between the settled farmers in the fertile lands, and the nomads of the desert – a feud recalled in Middle East warfare.

The next myth, that of the Nephilim, a commentary on a rebellious race of giants, leads to that of the Flood and Noah's Ark – one of the most popular of all time. Myths of great floods are current in every continent, both because floods have often happened, and because a flood aptly symbolizes individual disaster (Psalm 69;2), or mass destruction. One of the finest myths is the Gilgamesh epic, discovered in excavations at Nineveh, in the library of King Ashurbanipal (B.C. 668). As a myth, the resultant achievement is that of survival of the hero with his cherished possessions and the assurance of the god's protection. Noah's obedience to God, his construction of the ark, his survival, the rainbow signifying God's readiness to make a covenant or agreement, and to show mercy to the obedient, all these are familiar in Christian art.

The last of the timeless myths of human nature is the Tower of Babel. Its purpose is to explain the diversity of human languages, the existence of great ruins – in its biblical form a Ziggurat or temple tower in the Tigris valley – and as a commentary on the failure of great human endeavours.

The timeless myths of divine and human nature are succeeded by folklore. Folklore here means that body of traditional story, current amongst a people, which explains its origin and primitive history, often embodying primitive ideas as to various religious or moral problems. We enter the period of the sagas of Abraham, Isaac and Jacob. By sagas we mean stories long transmitted orally and preserving traditions of the wanderings of tribes and the exploits of heroes.

The great lesson of these sagas as seen by the compiler of Genesis, is the fact that God in time found it possible to trust certain men to obey His will and He could, thereafter, choose one nation to be the means by which He would in time invite all the nations back to Himself.

Like other ancient historical sources, the early biblical narratives sometimes simplify history by weaving it around one family which appears almost to be living on its own. This is so of the sagas of Abraham and his descendants. But, with the Old Testament narratives, the background can be supplied by excavation and by our knowledge of the conditions of Arabian nomadic life. Abraham and his tribe lived as the Bedawin in past ages and today, with no settled home, wandering from one oasis to another, leaving manual work to women, with simple food procured from the outskirts of civilization, joining with other families as occasion demanded, then separating again, united only by kinship, usually marrying only within their own tribe. Each family group had an autocratic head, who administered by custom and by tribal opinion.

Excavation gives much information about the life of Canaan in which and in whose desert surroundings the Patriarchs lived at the end of the early Bronze Age. Neolithic predecessors included a race of big people some of whom survived to the Patriarchial Age (Gen. 6;4, Num. 13;33), who may have built the megalithic monuments. These were the dolmens or large stones resting on upright stones, the menhirs or simple upright stones, and the gilgals or stone circles. Reference to tribal movements resembling those of the Patriarchs occurs in documents from Babylon in the time of Hammurabi (B.C. 1700, cf. Gen. 14) and in the Luxor Execration Texts.

Semite invasions about B.C. 3000 overran Palestine, established a dynasty in Babylon, and penetrated to Egypt, which recovered and spread her influence over Palestine. Later came the Canaanites; later still another movement of the Semites, of which the Exodus is an episode about B.C. 1225. The Canaanites ceased to wander, and built small towns and villages in which they lived a settled life, cultivating the vine and olive, digging water cisterns, and trading in pottery, gold ornaments, scarabs, etc. from Babylon and Egypt, using bronze and later iron for chariots. As the highway between Egypt and Babylon, Canaan was subject continually to one or other of these kingdoms. The Tel-el-Amarna tablets, written in Babylonian cuneiform, describe diplomatic communication between Egypt and Babylon. They refer on the one hand to the endless strife between native princes, and on the other to harassment from the Bedawin. They refer between c.B.C. 1400 and B.C. 1350 to the 'Habiru', a widespread, national name which also includes the Hebrews who under Joshua were invading Palestine about B.C. 1225.

Canaanite religion looked on certain places, stones or trees as sacred and gave to the deities who presided over them the titles of 'Baal' (lord, possessor) or 'El' (god). Their sacred places included the 'high places' such as pillars and tree stumps, which were originally phallic emblems. Their sacrifices included burnt offerings, and occasional child sacrifice.

It is in this setting that the Abraham saga is placed. Views vary as to the patriarch's dates, or even as to whether he is a historical person, or whether a number of events have been

The expulsion of Adam and Eve, Hans Acker, Ulm Cathedral.

traditionally attached to his name. But the activities in which he is concerned fit consistently with conditions of contemporary life in Palestine and summarize the advance in man's conception of the nature and will of God which took place at that time. Abraham is pictured as the ideal 'righteous man', the man of faith and obedience, whom God can use as the instrument for the fulfilment of His purposes of restoration.

In response to God's call, Abram (as he was at first called) left the rich city of Ur and became a nomad in Canaan and the desert around. Hunger drove him to Egypt, after which he returned to the desert. Excavation has revealed contemporary records of such journeys. He went to war with four Canaanite kings who were invading the territory of five kings near Sodom. He rescued his nephew Lot from them, in consequence of which took place the meeting with Melchizedek, king of Salem, that is, Jerusalem. There follows the ritual by which Abraham makes a covenant with God, and adopts the ancient Stone Age (Josh. 5;3) rite of circumcision as its symbol.

Following the destruction of Sodom come the Isaac sagas (which incorporate stories involving laughter – a play on the word Isaac, which means laughter). The most important of these is that of the sacrifice in Genesis 22, told in splendid Hebrew prose. 'After these things', that is, after a period of divine preparation, God tests Abraham to ascertain whether he is utterly loyal. The story dramatically builds up into a series of striking prefigurings of God's redemption of men in Christ; the father giving the son, the son doing the father's will, the symbols of sacrifice – the knife, the wood, the altar, the ram of the burnt offering – so God reveals what he will do for all men, through Abraham's offspring. Historically it appears as illustrating primite child sacrifice, giving way as man advances to animal sacrifice. Ethically the story supports the prophet Micah's protest against the long continuance of child sacrifice in Israel, 'Shall I give my firstborn for my transgression, the fruit of my body for the sin of my soul?' (Mic. 6;7). Finally, Abraham declares himself a pilgrim in the Land of Promise by buying – again in a story told in magnificent prose – the Cave of Machpelah from Ephron the Hittite, for a family burying place: and there it is to this day, goal of pilgrims, Jewish, Islam and Christians alike.

If Abraham typifies the ideal Israel, Jacob may be said to typify the real Israel, the Israel of history and of the prophets, continually sinning and suffering, yet ever seeking the birthright and the blessing. His birth and his rivalry with his brother Esau may be seen as mythically describing the struggle between the nations descended from them. Jacob obtains Esau's birthright for himself. He flees from Esau's wrath; wandering alone, he sleeps. He dreams of a ladder from earth to heaven; filled with awe, he calls the place Beth-El – house of God. He has learnt that God is interested in him and has a purpose for him. Later he struggles with an angel who appears to be God Himself (Gen. 32;24); he prevails over God and receives His blessing. Thus is mythically summarized the faith, and the fact that Israel's destiny is to survive where other nations decay. The faithful and the faithless will interpret the fact differently. None can deny it.

The tale of Jacob's wanderings mythologizes the history of the Habiru as revealed by recent research, and picturesque details like the angels on the ladder in his dream reflect local features like the ritual of the Ziggurat, that great Babylonian temple tower that must be climbed by the deified king as a token of the bond between heaven and earth.

The saga continues with Jacob settling in Canaan, and becoming the father of the twelve sons from whom the tribes of Israel – Jacob's new name, signifying his power with God – are descended. Recent evidence shows that political groups of six or twelve tribal units arose at an early stage amongst Middle East nations of the period. Again, genuine history is mythologized here.

The history of man's salvation continues with the story of Joseph (Gen. 37–50). Unlike the previous sagas, it is a consecutive narrative, working to a dramatic climax. Though it is difficult to fit it precisely with known Egyptian history, the details in the story fit closely with local conditions and betray intimacy with the land, whilst names like Jacob and Joseph exist in Egyptian records. Joseph's dreams excite the jealousy of his brothers, who take the opportunity of his visiting them, to sell him to Midianite merchants who take him to Egypt. He is sold to Potiphar, a royal official. Falsely accused by Potiphar's wife of attempted rape, he is imprisoned, where he interprets fellow prisoners' dreams. The Pharaoh or King hears of this, obtains from him interpretations of his own dreams, and is so impressed by his wisdom that he appoints him Grand Vizier of Egypt. His brothers come to buy food in time of famine and, after playing a deception game with them, he reveals the relationship and invites his father and brothers to come and live in Egypt. On Jacob's death the patriarch is taken in a coffin to the family tomb at Machpelah. Thus the way is paved for the next great act in the drama of the divine redemption of Israel – the Exodus from Egypt to Canaan.

The Bible's first book has described man's predicament, why he finds himself neither as God would have him be, nor as he would wish to be. The rest of the Bible tells how God rescued man from this. Exodus – 'the way out' – is a great new beginning in this process. Under Pharaoh Rameses II (in all probability) the Hebrews were degraded to slavery and efforts made to exterminate them. But there emerged a genius, born a Hebrew yet brought up at the Egyptian court, whose influence in leading his people from slavery to a national consciousness which they have never lost was so great, that Moses must be acknowledged a historic character. He is one of history's really great leaders – even if much of the literature and art concerned with his call, his interviews with Pharaoh, and the ten plagues may be unauthenticated.

Both the departure from Egypt and the entry to Canaan are facts of history. The stele of Merenptah states that in the fifth year of his reign (c.B.C. 1220) 'The people of Israel is desolate, it has no offspring. Palestine has become a widow for Egypt' (that is, has lost the power which protected it).

The simplest summary of the historic facts concerning Moses amounts to an achievement of world importance. He convinced the enslaved tribes in Egypt that Yahweh (the Hebrew name for God) cared for them and would deliver them. He led them to freedom and unity. He convinced them that *for them* (even if not as yet for the whole world) there must be one God, who, in making a covenant with his people, will demand their total loyalty. In general, he laid down the foundations of Israel's social, ceremonial and legal systems which, with many later developments, have survived the ages. He taught the Hebrews to believe in a God who was not a mere natural force, but was the personal cause of events, and to whom, as a moral being, men's actions have a moral importance. The faith of the psalms and the prophets is built on this teaching, and without its persistent influence there is no reason why Hebrew religion should have developed on a level so much higher than that of the Canaanites around.

To understand the reality enshrined in biblical mythology it is essential to realize that the record is set down to make plain God's purpose, rather than the policies of nations and rulers. It shows Israel's glory, not in its own achievements but in its being chosen by God. Successes are those of God, not of kings. Failures are remedial discipline.

The account of Moses' death (Deut. 34) on a mountain top, not in the promised land but with a magnificent view of it from end to end, tells in superb prose of the vision granted to a dying leader, of the permanent value of his work. He will not share it, but he foresees it. The view, easy of access to the traveller, permits him, in a sense, to share the vision today.

The Hebrews are described in the Bible as entering the Promised Land under the leadership of Joshua. It may be impossible today to be sure that many of the incidents of the conquest are anything but traditional fables in their present form. There can be no doubt that, broadly speaking, the entry of the Hebrews – probably over a longer period than the book of Joshua envisages – and their assimilation of Canaanite agricultural religion with its sacred sites, associating them with Yahweh, rather as early Christian missionaries built churches on pagan sites, are facts of history. For a long time social conditions were simple, 'cities' were small; we should call them villages. Stories in the books of Joshua, Judges, Ruth and Samuel illustrate features of such life as seen through the eyes of their writers. There was as yet no administrative unity 'Every man did what was right in his own eyes'. The local judges would lead in emergency. Canaanite attacks and those of other tribes were frequent. The land was largely dominated by Philistines – probably immigrants from Crete after the destruction of its Minoan civilization, who brought the use of iron and of the Phoenecian alphabet (replacing Babylonic cuneiform) to the Israelites.

Guilds of prophets began at this period. They were crude and simple at first, but prophecy was destined to become a movement of the greatest importance to the world. Its first outstanding personality was Samuel. His great achievement was to seize on the people's desire for freedom from the Philistines, to preach obedience to Yahweh which would result in national unity. This was based on the inspiration of Yahweh who was to remain the one and only God of Israel and whose nature later prophets would reveal ever more gloriously.

Samuel hoped for national unity under God alone, but the people demanded a king. Samuel, having warned them what this would mean, and believing that he was acting with divine authority, anointed Saul as king, thus using the method of hallowing the monarch, traditional ever since and still used at the coronation of English monarchs. Kingship developed quickly under David and Solomon; like other advanced societies, the Jewish kingdom acquired money for its government, a court with officials and, above all, the temple as the shrine of national inspiration, memories and hopes. It had an army and an organized system of justice. It boasted of a developed form of city life in Jerusalem, Samaria and elsewhere, while commerce and an increasing variety of trades and occupations flourished throughout the land. However, with these new sophistications of life came a general moral deterioration with an increasing gulf between rich and poor. A greater awareness of culture, including literature, developed, while pottery, jewellery, music, architecture and engineering made great advances. Remains from this period include ivory carvings from King Ahab's 'ivory palace' at Samaria, and Hezekiah's tunnel at Jerusalem which still conveys water as of old – but the writers recall such matters merely in the form of footnotes (1 kings 22;39, 2 Kings 20;20) and as of little permanent interest compared with the development of God's purpose.

Diplomatic connections with other kingdoms brought alien religious practices to the land, and kingship came to mean oppression. Such causes led to the great development of the prophetic movement. Prophecy's real achievement is the proclaiming of the nature of God and goodness, leading to the hope that God will one day act once and for all for the salvation of men. The popular modern conception of 'foretelling the future' in political and other directions is a less important implication.

After Moses the eighth century prophets of Israel embody that country's supreme contribution to history. They lifted up the conception of Israel's God from being the national hero who fought for it against its enemies, to become the one God of all the earth. They raised the divine conception from one of aweful power to pure goodness, demanding goodness from His followers in the shape of social justice, mercy, humility and love. Elijah and Elisha claimed that Yahweh of Israel and Baal of Tyre cannot be worshipped together. Amos emphasized Yahweh's righteousness and justice, and His rule over all the nations; Hosea spoke of His love and mercy; Isaiah and Michah emphasized His aweful purity; Zephaniah foretold the day of judgment; Jeremiah emphasized individual religion and personal responsibility to Yahweh. Nahum proclaimed Nineveh's doom whilst Jonah was led to see that God is merciful to all nations, including even Nineveh. In general, they taught no longer that what is good is nationally right, but that what is right is nationally good.

The prophetic teaching was in its time so new that it was not popular. Under King Manasseh the prophets were silenced. They 'went underground' and wrote their main tenets in a book, the core of Deuteronomy. Under King Josiah (B.C. 639), this was discovered in the Temple. The book maintains that 'The Lord our God is *one* Lord' – Yahweh is the

Moses reads God's commands to the people, misericord, Worcester, see pg 30.

universal God. He must have only one place of worship; heathen shrines must go. The great annual feasts, Passover, Weeks (Pentecost) and Tabernacles, formerly agricultural, must have a spiritual character. There must be only one priesthood, that of the tribe of Levi. On this book Josiah based national reformation, short lived at the time, but exerting influence later on.

Not long afterwards, in B.C. 587, Jerusalem fell. The Jewish exile in Babylon began, and with it began the world-wide dispersion of the Jews, which has continued ever since. The effects of the dispersion are obvious today. The Jews, unable to practise their religion in their own land, have made it a worldwide faith. Many of them acquired important positions, such as that of Daniel at the Babylonian court, and their worldwide commercial instinct and practice began. Although the majority settled in their new homes, the hope of return never left them. After the fall of Babylon in B.C. 538, a number did return, and the priestly state which they set up lasted, under domination by Persia, Greece, Syria and Rome until A.D. 70. It was in this state that Jesus Christ was born and lived.

The main features of religion under the high priests were an insistence on the holiness of God, man's need to pay God reverence, the fearfulness of sin and the need for atonement in order to be made 'at one' with God again, emphasized in the ritual of the Day of Atonement, and the necessity of exact observance of the Sabbath and of the Law, for God, they thought, was so utterly removed from man that the most man could hope to do was to keep the Law.

The sense of the isolated holiness of God led to the Jewish form of belief in angels. In earlier days 'the angel of the Lord' had had a vague and varied meaning. It often was a picturesque way of describing the Lord Himself. But, perhaps under Persian influence, Judaism developed an ordered system of archangels and angels, as described in Tobit 12; 15. With this there developed belief in evil spirits, as in Zechariah 3; 1; they were sometimes thought of as evil angels, cf. Job 1;6.

Finally, it was at this time that there developed two beliefs of outstanding importance, that of the Messiah or Anointed One who would come and restore the nation to its ideal state, and that of the immortality of the individual – in the Book of the Wisdom of Solomon 1; 13–15, life for the good and punishment for the wicked. This new doctrine was supported by the Pharisees – the strictly orthodox followers of the *Torah* – and opposed by the Sadducees, who denied the existence of angels and spirits.

The centuries of preparation from Abraham onwards, thus led to a dynamic sense of hope and expectancy, coming to fulfilment in the New Testament. A W F Blunt in *Israel: Social and Religious Development** brilliantly summarizes the fulfilment of this hope:

> The central movement of vital religion in Judaism was carried on into Christianity, which inherits and enriches all the best elements contained in the prophetic teaching, and becomes the inspiration of the higher thought of the western world. In the Christian doctrine of the Trinity we find a conception of God which preserves the fundamental truth of Monotheism, while saving monotheistic belief from that cold Deism which places God far off from men in an existence of bare isolation. Jeremiah's conception of indi-

vidual inner religion, of the 'law in the heart', finds its fulfilment in the Christian doctrine of the Holy Spirit. The Jewish attempt to unite sacrificial observance with mystic communion at last achieves success in the Christian Eucharist. The prophetic universalism finds a term of accomodation with the human craving for a visible organization, in the gospel conception of 'the Kingdom of God'. The thought of the lovingness of Yahweh expands into our Lord's revelation of 'our Father in heaven', of a God who, though infinitely high, is yet indefinitely near, of a God who is no longer merely loving, but who is, in Himself and essentially, Love, the love which shows its perfect quality in the Cross of Jesus Christ, where the divine Love reveals itself as a love eternally ready to suffer with man and for his salvation.

The New Testament follows naturally from the Old Testament, not supplanting it but, for Christians, fulfilling it. The alienation which through the centuries has been fostered between holders of the Jewish faith and Christians is largely based on the fact that the former refuse to accept the divine nature of Christ. Yet every New Testament book, save the Gospel of St Luke, was, in all probability, written by Jews. The central theme of Jesus teaching – the Kingdom of God – develops that of the prophets' teaching. It may be salutary to remember that a large proportion of Christian worship and Christian art consists of and derives from Old Testament writings. Jesus summed up the relationship of Old and New, thus: 'Do not suppose that I have come to abolish the law and the prophets. I did not come to abolish, but to complete' (Matt. 5;17).

Before embarking on a brief survey of the New Testament's theme – the coming of Jesus Christ – it is necessary to summarize briefly some preliminary matters.

The Life of Jesus of Nazareth during the first century of our era, in the small turbulent Jewish province of the Roman Empire, is a fact of history. Anyone who attempts to treat Him as a ficticious fabrication is simply attempting to bypass one of the facts of life. Nor is it possible to dismiss Him on grounds that He lived in a distant age of which we know little. The circumstances of the time in which He lived can become familiar to all who wish to investigate them. Articles in Peake's *Commentary on the Bible* by scholars of repute, on the Jewish state in the Hellenistic world, on Judaism in the Greek and Roman periods, on the Roman Empire in the first century, on contemporary Jewish religion, and on pagan religion at the coming of Christianity, with the numerous scholarly books there quoted, put Jesus's coming into its historically correct context, with which the alleged origins of many modern deviationist sects bear no comparison.

But, secondly, the life of Jesus was no ordinary life. He claimed a unique relationship with God, His 'Father'. He acknowledged Himself to be the Messiah or Anointed One of prophecy, with authority above that of Jewish high priest or Roman emperor, and it was for this claim that He was crucified. The impact which He made on those of His contemporaries who were capable of appreciating Him was such that they greeted Him either with fear and deadly hostility, or with wholehearted loyalty leading eventually to a spirit of triumph which nothing could destroy. Ordinary and familiar and attractive as He might appear in daily life, there was yet something about Him, deeply mysterious, dynamic and irresistible, which convinced both friends and foes that He was 'otherworldly'.

It follows from this, that although He was seen with men's

---

*A W F Blunt, *Israel: Social and Religious Development*, OUP 1924.

eyes and heard with men's ears, it was beyond men's power to describe in ordinary terms all that they perceived in Him, and all that in their later thought flowed from their experience of Him. Their witness to His resurrection, to His post resurrection appearances, to His ascension, and to the coming of His spirit and all that has flowed from this, defy description in human terms for we do not fully understand them. But it does not follow from this that these events have no meaning today. It is relevant to note here that each significant advance in science leads to further mysteries unsolved, and to further dilemmas as to behaviour. Man on his own is out of his depth today as in the past. Man today, as in the past, is wise to accept such mysteries partially disclosed to him as can guide him to firm ground in his search for truth and wisdom.

Once men had come to frame language to attempt to convey the meaning of Jesus to them, there began the new and endless process of transmitting it to people of other races, times and places. The purpose of those who undertook this was 'in order that you may hold the faith that Jesus is the Christ, the Son of God, and that through this faith you may possess eternal life by His name' (Jn 20;21). They did not give us a biography of Jesus, nor descriptions of His character or appearance, and the social conditions He shared only enter incidentally. At first, incidents were repeated from mouth to mouth, and no doubt learnt by heart, based on some important saying, with the event leading up to it. As time passed, the stories became more detailed. Comparison between Mark, the first and simplest Gospel we possess, written between A.D. 65 and A.D. 70; Matthew written a few years later and incorporating the majority of Mark with much additional material; Luke, thought to have been written about A.D. 80 (also incorporating Markan passages), and John, written about A.D. 90, shows how details increase with the passage of time. Repetition and learning of the simplest 'forms' as they are usually called, would have begun, probably in Aramaic, as soon as the words and deeds had taken place.

Writing could well have followed very soon afterwards; certainly Luke would be likely to have worked up his travel diary of events in which he shared in Acts 16 onwards, as soon as possible.*

The vast majority of these early, polyracial Christians directed their energies towards sharing their life of worship, serving others, caring for those in need, extending the Christian Church to yet other races and creeds, and, in their earliest days, preparing for Christ's expected second coming.

By far the most outstanding early follower of Jesus was the Jew, Saul of Tarsus later called Paul. A leading Pharisee who became an ardent persecutor of the Christians, his sudden conversion to the Faith (with his change of name to Paul) is one of the outstanding events in world history. Thereafter he spent his life in the spreading of the faith and the organizing of the Church, to which ends he devoted unflagging energy, and in whose cause he underwent great sufferings culminating in his probable martyrdom in Rome in about A.D. 64. His letters to his fellow Christians were written between A.D. 48 (the letter to the Galatians) and A.D. 64(?) (the second letter to Timothy). They form the earliest source of information about the Good News which the apostles were preaching in the Church's early days, and have become an important part of Christian doctrine.

In brief, the content of the Good News is as follows: God,

in the fulness of time and in accordance with prophecy, has sent His son Jesus Christ, who was bron of King David's line, lived under the Law, taught God's truth and by his death redeemed others from the curse incurred by sin. He was betrayed and crucified by men and buried. He was raised again by God on the third day. He appeared to many witnesses. He was exalted to a place of power and glory at God's right hand. He will appear to judge the world, to consummate for His people the salvation He has won for them, and will bring lasting bliss to all creation.

Outstanding passages in Paul's letters include: 1 Corinthians 15, a description of how Christ's death and resurrection took place 'in accordance with the scriptures. Risen, He appeared to many people, including 500 witnesses at once "most of whom are still alive"'. In 1 Corinthians 11;23 is to be found the earliest existing account of the institution of the Holy Eucharist. In Philippians 2;5–11 we read a description of Christ's

Pentecost, 11th century mosaic, Greece, see pg 64.

humiliation and exaltation. In Romans 13;14 we are told to 'put on the Lord Jesus Christ' that is, allow Him to radically change our whole behaviour. In Colossians 3;5–4;6 we are given an extended form of ethical teaching for newly converted Christians.

The extraordinary power of persuasion of Paul's letters is demonstrated by their effect on Augustine the sinner who became Bishop of Hippo and a saint (*Confessions* 8;29), on Martin Luther the German monk, on John Wesley, the English Methodist preacher and hymn writer and on countless others through the centuries to the present day.

Soon after the death of Paul and of Peter the Apostle, during the persecution of Christians under Nero, there began the writing of the Gospels in their present form. This may have been prompted by the diffusion of believers in most of the major cities and ports of Asia Minor, by their persecution, and by the realization that the meaning of Christ's coming should be recorded in order to prepare for the time when the Apostles with their first hand witness would no longer be alive.

Whilst the Gospels follow naturally upon the Old Testament, it should be noted that there are important contrasts between the Old Testament and the New. Whilst the Old Testament is the result of the work of many writers over many centuries, and incorporates a wide variety of literature, the New Testament books were all written within 50 years, between about A.D. 50 and A.D. 100, by a few writers, and within anything from 18 to 70 years of the events of which they treat. The New Testament books were written, not to record a distant past, but for the use of the young and growing Christian Church and for the enriching of its corporate life and worship.

Christianity was not 'the faith of a book', but was and is the shared life of a community that believes itself redeemed, and the fact that so many individuals can find so much of value in the New Testament bears witness to the power of Christ in His Church.

We turn now to a very brief summary of the life and teaching of Jesus. For anything like a worthy knowledge of Him sufficient to enable one to declare one's belief or disbelief, it is necessary to read the four Gospels. This is best done in the order in which they were written, supplemented by scholarly explanatory matter such as is found in 'The Life and Teaching of Jesus' in Peake's *Commentary*, and in the books there cited. Mark, the writer of the first Gospel, sketches a bare outline of Christ's life and death. Matthew, concerned to persuade the Jews that Jesus was indeed their long-awaited Messiah, gives Christ's descent from Abraham through David, while Luke, mainly presenting Jesus to the non-Jew records this descent from Adam as the common ancestor of all men. John tells of The eternal Word: of the power and love of God, made man.

John the Baptist, the 'great forerunner', baptizes Jesus, upon whom, declared by God to be His Son, comes the Holy Spirit in a unique way. Withdrawing to meditate on His call, He is tempted to disobedience, distrust, and disloyalty. He resists. Henceforth His life is one of unique authority, service, and obedience to His Father's will.

With John the Baptist's arrest, Jesus begins in Galilee His ministry which is to end on the cross, with the words 'The time is fulfilled and the Kingdom of God is at hand; repent and believe the Gospel'. In brief, He is saying that God, our Father, is near at hand, it is for us to hear His call through His Messiah, and to accept His reign in their hearts; such acceptance can revolutionize life in all its aspects. He expands

this call with parables, poems, and sermons, designed to illustrate the spirit of sympathy, gentleness, service, sacrifice, humility, forgiveness, compassion, purity, faith, honesty, courage, love, and other virtues, which mark those in the Kingdom, together with the cost which membership demands. His teaching also included condemnation of those who by their legalism and hypocracy distort men's understanding of God.

It is unnecessary to worry about Jesus' miracles. The greatest miracle of all was Jesus Himself, His spirit, His message, His eternal triumph in men's hearts. The miracles follow naturally, as local and temporal manifestations, of response to local and temporal needs. They might strengthen the faithful. They were not intended to convince the doubters and the scornful.

The early impact of the ministry in the Galilean countryside was one of overwhelming popularity. But the Kingdom could not rest on popularity alone. As the Gospel must be given by God incarnate – that is, 'in the flesh' – so the Gospel must be lived in community – by people together – and the divine community must have divine sanction. So to the climax of the ministry – Jesus asks the twelve disciples whom He had chosen for special training, 'Who do men say I am?' Peter, who is their natural leader, replies, 'You are the Messiah' (Mk 8;29). Once they realize His unique position, He can found His Church on this belief (Matt. 16;18), and He can prepare them for men's great rejection of Him, a rejection His followers must be prepared to share. There follows the vision of Him preparing to fulfil the Law and the Prophets (Lk. 9;30). His teaching becomes more and more dynamic, more and more fundamental. He is to come to glory through suffering. He is Lord of all and Servant of all. His final triumph will be in violent death and in conquest of death. His Church must follow His example.

So to Jesus's Passion: the climax of His life, of the history of His nation, and of the history of all humanity. He sets His face towards Jerusalem, city of love and hatred, city of God yet city which kills the prophets, there to experience the week upon which the central Gospel of Paul and of the Church is based. He lives this week, the sure master of events. All happens with tremendous inevitability. He is the Victor.

He rides into Jerusalem, a king of peace. He is anointed at supper at Bethany, 'for His burial'. During the last week He challenges the Temple authorities by driving out their merchants; this intensifies the hostility which is to end in His death. He is involved in bitter controversy with the Pharisees, the strict adherers to the Jewish law, and King Herod's followers on matters of fundamental importance. He speaks of the end of time, the birth pangs of the new age, the need to be watchful for its coming, and the inevitability of judgment. – His words in Matthew 25;31–46 are recalled in the innumerable 'Doom' or 'Last Judgment' paintings once over the chancel arch of every parish church, and frequently still in this position and in the west window or over the great west door. On Thursday the secretly prepared Last Supper takes place, with the sharing of the bread: 'My Body, broken for you', and of the wine: 'My Blood, shed for you', thus uniting the Passover from the ancient past with the forthcoming great Rejection in the betrayal, the trials and the crucifixion, while finally both are transcended with the triumphant sharing of the Risen Christ in all ages which are to come.

All is fulfilled. He is betrayed. He is tried by the religious leaders of His nation. In rejecting Him they seal their nation's doom. He is tried by the Roman Governor. In failing and in washing his hands of the matter, he demonstrates the weakness of temporal power. He is taken to Calvary and nailed to the cross. And here He shows His final glory. He dies with a shout of triumph 'It is accomplished!'. For ever after, the cross

St Paul and St Peter, 5th century mosaic, Ravenna, see Pg 68.

stands as the inspiration of the victory of self sacrifice in the cause of right, but supremely it shows God acting to save men.

The triumph of love over hate and life over death is completed. The God of Life raises Him up. Again and again He meets with His friends, and leads them to understand how they will soon cease to see Him with their eyes – for this implies a presence limited to one place at a time – and they will instead know that He will be with them unseen and everywhere, like the air we breathe. Their last sight of Him convinces them that this is so. Here cold scientific language fails. For this is the ultimate mystery of life, where the temporal and the finite meet the eternal and the infinite. So we talk of the Resurrection and the Ascension. We do not understand the full meaning of these words, but we believe they describe facts, which reveal truth of vital importance to all humanity, for they tell us about our being and our future.

In this faith the young Church went forth, as described in the Acts of the Apostles, in the power of the Spirit of God – again the language of myth and mystery, but again conveying fact revealing truth.

The Acts of the Apostles bridges the gap between mystery and modern life. So much of it seems close to us. Archaeology has brought many of the places mentioned into the light of our days. We can see today the places which Paul and Luke and the others saw. We can face the problems they faced, meet the kind of people they met – and yet they are so clearly moving 'in the power of the Spirit', their lives are carried forward by a superhuman power. Visions and miracles are part of their daily scene. Paul's life, in particular, moves forward with a kind of powerful inevitability. And, just as Mark's Gospel ends with a sentence torn in two, so The Acts ends with a startling suddenness – like a Greek Orthodox Eucharist – which leaves one suspended in the grip of movement forward into total fulfilment.

We have nearly finished our brief survey of the Bible. We began with the myths and mysteries of the distant past. We finish with those of the future, in the Book of Revelation also called the Apocalypse, the Bible's last book. It is one of a group of such books, written in times of stress, to comfort their readers by showing that suffering must come, but that all will be well in the end. It is the finest Christian example of its type. It develops, almost like grand music, in three movements – Christ sends messages to the Seven Churches, God judges His enemies and gives victory to the faithful, and God's kingdom comes on earth. It is in part, clearly a meditation during a Christian Eucharist. One should if possible read it in a Byzantine Church. It forms a link between the written word and the artistic representation of the House of God, it echoes the marching forward of the Christian liturgy, the marching forward of the calendar of the Church, from Advent through Christmas, the Epiphany, Lent, Good Friday, Easter, Ascension, Whitsunday, and the other Holy days, shared by the worshippers who are constantly reminded of all these truths; it is reflected in the mosaics, the wall paintings, the sculptures, the glass, while the whole is fused into the glory from floor to roof of the building alive with worship.

The Genesis Stories

Left
The Creation of the sun and moon on the fourth day. According to Genesis, God created the sun and the moon for the sole purpose of giving light to the earth and to man. In Hebrew imagination the picture of God's universe was one of heaven above and hell below, with terrestrial man poised between the divine and demonic forces of each. The act of creation, as recounted in Genesis, took place in six days, a mystic and sacred number among Egyptians and Babylonians too. Detail of the Creation from the Chapter House, Salisbury Cathedral, 13th century.

Right
The Creation of heaven and earth. Fire is descending from a white sphere and God controls it with a large pair of compasses. Christian art interprets the Bible and the teachings of the Church in the simplest terms, often with picturesque details out of the artist's imagination. These two stained glass windows are from a 15th century series at Great Malvern Priory which starts with the creation theme.

Right
God creates the animals. According to Genesis, all living matter was formed out of earth or clay. 'And out of the ground the Lord God made every beast of the field and every fowl of the air, and brought them to Adam, to see what he would call them. And whatever name Adam gave each living creature, it was called that' (Genesis 2;19). The act of naming is a very important symbol. It is creative, second only to begetting life. To know the name of a person or thing is to to have power over it and therefore responsibility – a matter of crucial importance today.

The backgrounds in the Malvern windows imitate tapestries perhaps derived from the back cloths of the mystery plays. Some of the designs are of earlier date, taken from a 14th century book *Speculum Humanae Salvationis*. The animals in particular are lively and lifelike. The series is a proud demonstration of the newly invented 'yellow stain' made by painting silver nitrate on white glass.

Left and below
The Serpent tempts Adam and Eve; God expels them from Paradise. God made man from the earth, and breathed life and immortality into him, we are told in Genesis. In the related myth of Mohammedan tradition, God takes seven handfuls of earth from different depths and of different colours for the creation of Adam, to account for our racial disparities. God places Adam in the Garden of Eden, meaning a place of delight and pleasure. He lives there, filled with wisdom and beauty, and innocent of power or of evil. Then, in one of the profoundest images of the Old Testament, God creates woman out of Adam's own body. 'And Adam called her *Eve*, which means *the mother of all things*'. Her image is of the greatest importance, for she is to be the bearer of life. The rich language of the symbols used here draws heavily from ancient Semitic mythology, to present the human tragedy. Adam and Eve live in Paradise, to give it its Persian name. They are allowed to eat of every fruit in the garden, except that of the trees of forbidden knowledge and of immortal life. The symbols we find used here run through the whole of Christian scripture. In these early myths the knowledge of good and evil means the knowledge of spells and of incantations through which the powers of darkness could be summoned and controlled. In Hebrew tradition it was the serpent who had this knowledge of magic. He tempts Eve, telling her that to eat the fruit will make her independent of God. Adam and Eve disobey God; they eat the fruit. With the knowledge of good and evil their innocence is taken from them; their relationship with God is broken. They are banished from Eden; instead of a loving closeness to the things that grow out of the soil, Adam now must struggle to make it fertile, while Eve's fertility is accompanied by pain and, sometimes, death. They see the functions of their bodies as things of shame; man by his disobedience to the divine will has marred what God made.

The theme of the Fall is richly depicted in Christian art. At a time when few men could read and copies of the Bible were handwritten and in a foreign language (Latin), people's religious knowledge was based on what they could see illustrated in their churches. The artists too did not often consult the original source, and so the unspecified 'fruit' of Genesis gradually establishes itself as an apple by medieval times. The picture *left* depicts Adam and Eve's temptation by the serpent as interpreted by Hans Acker in 1420. The serpent is crowned, symbolizing him as the fount of wisdom – the glass window is to be found in the Besserer Chapel, Ulm Cathedral. *Below*, relief from Andlau Church, Alsace, c.1080–1100.
Following page
Adam and Eve's temptation and subsequent expulsion; below 11th–12th century bronze doors, St Zeno's Basilica, Verona. *Above* shows the expulsion of Adam and Eve on a 14th century misericord, Worcester Cathedral. Adam and Eve are here depicted in a characteristic pose of the 'anti-type' tableaux for a passion play.

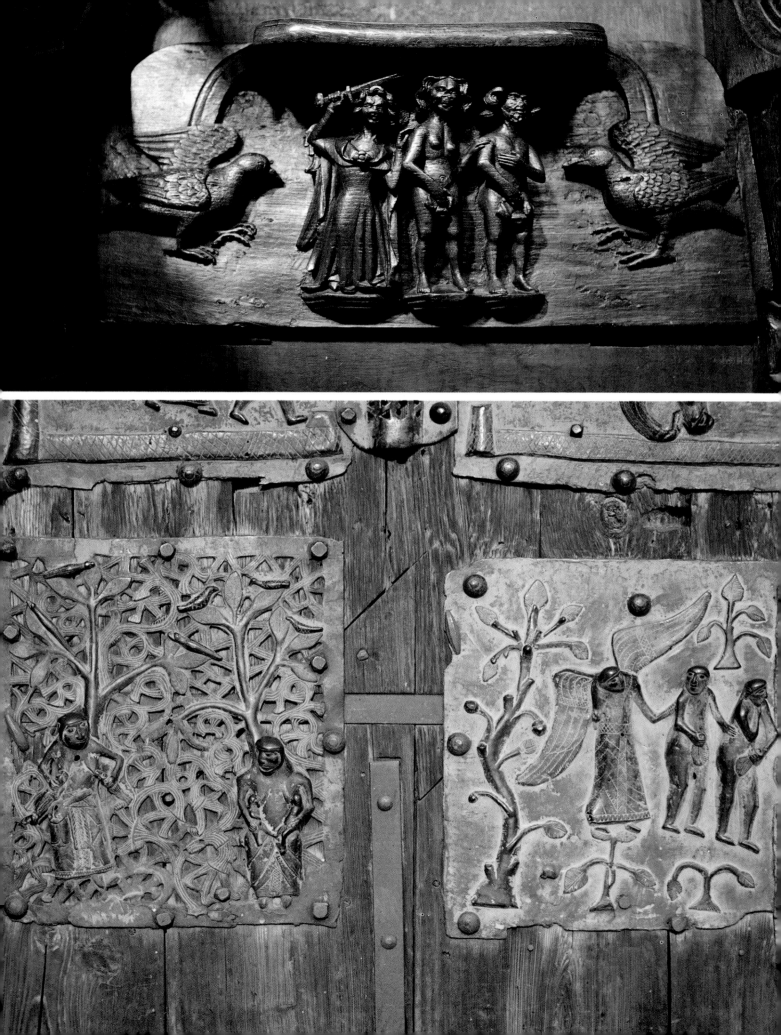

Above left
Cain murders his brother Abel. These two sons of Eve work as farmer and shepherd respectively, until the former is filled with jealousy of his brother and kills him. God is angry with him, and condemns him to a life of wandering. This Old Testament version of a much earlier myth attempts to explain the two different types of community of the ancient world; the pastoral and the agricultural. Each offers its ritual sacrifice to God for the fertility of its crops, but the farmer believes that God's benevolence is directed towards his brother alone. In the earlier myths the killing is justified by a ritual ceremony to fertilize the soil by drenching it with the blood of his victim. As in the related myths of Babylon and Greece, the slayer flees, protected by God's mark to indicate his sacred character. The interpretation given to this by the compiler of Genesis is that with this first death man removes himself further still from God. The consequences are disastrous, for Cain builds a city and founds a society without God (Genesis. 4;17). Cain in the act of murdering his brother; from a Romanesque capital, San Juan de la Peña, Navarre.

Above
Lamoch's accidental killing of Cain 'I kill a man for wounding me, a young man for a blow' (Genesis 4;23) was explained by a Jewish legend. Lamoch, old and blind, took his son Tubalcain to direct the aim of his bow. Seeing movement in some bushes, Tubalcain told Lamoch to shoot, but the victim was found to be Cain. 12th century capital, Autun Cathedral.

Left
The creation of Eve (above), and the dove returning to Noah in the ark (below). 'And the Lord God caused a deep sleep to fall on Adam, and he slept. And he took one of his ribs, and closed his body again. And out of the rib, which God had taken from the man, he made a woman, and brought her to the man.' (Genesis 2; 21–23). An initial from the illuminated Winchester Bible, 12th century.

The myth of Noah. Noah means 'comfort', for he shows by his survival of the flood that God has mercy on the man who obeys Him. There are various accounts of the flood in Sumerian, Babylonian and Semitic myths which may have been inspired by a folk-memory of severe local flooding. The excavations of Ur and of other ancient Mesopotamian cities show evidence of destruction by water at a very early date. In all these myths God gives specific instructions for the building of the ark, which ranges from three to seven storeys in height, and is made watertight with pitch. In a symbolic picture of the consequences of the rejection of God by man the survivors of the ark see the order that had been established at the creation of the world break down before their eyes while the earth is submerged under darkness and chaos. When order is restored, God assures Noah that He will not curse the earth again for man's sake, and He leaves him the rainbow as a sign of covenant. Thus the Genesis story offers both an explanation for the phenomenon of the rainbow and introduces it as a symbol of divine mercy.

Top left the myth as depicted in the Chapter House of Salisbury Cathedral, 1275, with Noah receiving the dove and the raven into the ark.

Below left the animals enter the ark; Great Malvern Priory; 15th century.

Right
Noah is seen receiving the dove back into the ark. Besserer Chapel, Ulm; 15th century.

Left
The shame of Noah. Noah becomes a farmer; he grows grapes, makes wine and lies drunken in his tent (Genesis 9;21). His son Ham sees him lying naked and tells his brothers Shem and Japheth. They cover him with a cloak. Noah curses Canaan, Ham's son, and blesses Shem and Japheth, whose slave Canaan is to become. With this myth the compiler of Genesis shows that even after the lesson of the flood man remains the same. He abuses God's good gift of the vine, and father turns against son. Great Malvern Priory; 15th century.

Left above right
The building of the Tower of Babel (Genesis 11;1–9). Man in his vanity attempts to build a tower that will reach up to God Himself. But God confounds him, and scatters him over the earth. Worse, each man now speaks a different language, so that the understanding that God gave us through the spoken word is lost for ever. In this myth we have an attempt to explain the existence of different languages. It shows in symbolic terms not only the final stage in the disintegration of order and unity as created by God at the beginning of time, but also the conflict of interests inevitable when men try to rule themselves without the inspiration of a superhuman force of unity. Chapter House, Salisbury Cathedral; 13th century.

The First Israelites

21

Left
Abel and Melchizedek make their offering to God
(Genesis 4:4 & Genesis 14;18). Abel gives a
lamb from his flock as a sacrifice to ensure
God's continued blessing on him. Melchizedek, priest-king of Salem (Jerusalem)
offers bread and wine in thanksgiving for
Abraham's victory over invaders from the
east. Both acts were of deep symbolic significance and foreshadow the sacrificial
nature of Christ. Mosaic in the Church of
San Vitale, Ravenna, 6th century.

Below
Abraham entertains the three angels of God
(Genesis 18;8). Abraham is childless and old,
yet God says that he is to be the father of
many nations. He sends three messengers
who tell the old man that his wife Sarah is
to bear him a son. The son is to be called
Isaac, a name meaning laughter. In
Abraham, God has found a man of faith
and obedience through whom mankind may
be led back to its favoured relationship with
the creator. The long, slow pilgrimage of
man back to God has begun. Wall painting,
Church of the Archangel Michael, Galata,
Cyprus; 16th century.

Above
Angels lead Lot and his daughters to safety while Lot's wife looks back. In this myth we are again told of the destruction of man as a result of his disobedience to God. The twin cities of Sodom and Gomorrah are filled with vice and immorality, and must consequently be wiped off the face of the earth. In this picture fire and brimstone can be seen raining from the skies upon Sodom. Lot and his children escape, but his wife, who disobeys God and turns back to see his judgement is turned into a pillar of salt. To this day rocks of salt may be seen near the Dead Sea where a sudden subsistence of land is said to have accounted for the destruction of the cities. Canterbury Cathedral; 13th century.

Top right
The destruction of Sodom (Genesis 19; 24–25). 'And Abraham said to God, "Will you destroy the good as well as the wicked?"

And God replied, "If I find in Sodom fifty good men I will spare all for their sake'. And Abraham said, "If you have all but five of these good men, will you destroy the city?" "If I have all but five, I will not destroy it". Here man confronts his God on a new level of moral awareness and responsibility. We are told that God created man in his own image, and in Abraham this likeness begins to be revealed. Frieze, Salisbury Cathedral; 13th century.

Right
Abraham offering Isaac for sacrifice. He is told to build an altar in the mountains and prepare his son as the sacrificial victim. The child, whom God had given him must, he believes, be returned to God as a token of his absolute obedience to the divine will. But God stays his hand in the act, and the son's life is spared. Instead, Abraham kills the ram that is caught in the thicket, thus transferring the symbol of sacrifice. There is

clear evidence that in early Hebrew worship some children were, as the tribe's most precious possession, sacrificed and burnt on the altar of God. Similarly, we find the Carthaginians sacrificing their children to Moloch and the Cretans to the Minotaur. Indeed, the symbol of offering a human life as the supreme sacrifice is so deep-rooted in man that at one time or another it has been practiced almost universally. So we find that Western man, by accepting the death of Christ as the apex of all sacrifice, also accepts that he himself must 'die into life' before he can attain self-knowledge. The details of the stained glass window build up into a dramatic prefiguring of the Cross, where the wood is arranged in the shape of a cross and Isaac is bound to it. Canterbury Cathedral, 13th century.

Following page. The same scene, Church of the Holy Cross, Platanistasa, Cyprus; 15th century.

Below
Jacob's Ladder. Fleeing from the anger of his brother Esau, Jacob sinks down exhausted in the desert. 'And he took the stones of that place and put them for his pillows, and lay down in that place to sleep. And he dreamed, and behold a ladder set up on the earth, and the top of it reached to heaven: and behold the angels of God ascending and descending on it.'
In this picture the 'ladder' consists of a flight of steps rising in a curve, resembling the stone staircases to the 'high places' at Petra and the ziggurats. (Genesis 28; 11–12). Kariye Camii, Istanbul; 14th century.

Right
Jacob's Dream. 'And behold, the Lord said, I am the Lord God of Abraham thy father, and the God of Isaac. The land whereon thou liest, to thee will I give it, and to thy seed; And thy seed shall be as the dust of the earth, and thou shalt spread abroad to the west, and to the east, and to the north, and to the south: and in thee and in thy seed shall all the families of the earth be blessed.' (Genesis 28; 13–14). Here Jacob's dream is shown, rather than his actual posture asleep, for he stands and is greeted by the angel of the Lord. Salisbury Cathedral, 13th century.

Below right
Jacob wrestles with the angel. After years in exile, Jacob returns to his own people. He rests alone by the river Jabbok and night falls. Suddenly he feels a presence by his side. He is afraid and, standing in the shallow stream, locks himself against the other in a struggle that lasts all night. *cont.*

continued from previous page
As dawn breaks Jacob cries out for a blessing. He is released and his opponent is revealed as God Himself. From now on Jacob's name is 'Israel', for he has wrestled with God and with men and has prevailed. Church of St Mary Magdelene, Vezelay, France; 12th century.

Above
Joseph interpreting Pharaoh's dream. Jacob's sons are jealous of their father's favourite, Joseph. He barely escapes with his life, and spends many years in Egypt, first as a slave, then as a prisoner. But through his remarkable powers of dream devination he is restored to a place of high authority at Pharaoh's court. Note the technique used in this 17th century Flemish church window. The glass is 'enamelled'; white glass is used, with the colours painted directly on to it. This dispenses with the need to lead separate colours together, and makes smaller and more detailed pictures possible. Wells Cathedral; 17th century.

Top right
Joseph's cup found in Benjamin's sack. Jacob's sons are stricken by the famine that rages in Canaan. They go to Egypt to fill their sacks with corn and are recognized by their brother Joseph, who is now governor of Egypt. In order to persuade them to bring their father Jacob to Egypt, he takes Benjamin in custody, accusing him falsely of stealing a silver cup away in his corn sack. At last the family is reunited. Jacob and his twelve sons return to Egypt and the history of the nation of Israel may begin. Misercord, Amiens Cathedral; 16th century.

Right
Joseph greets Jacob his father. Jacob, now an old man, is persuaded to leave the safety of his refuge in Canaan and travel to Egypt. Here he meets his long-lost son. 'And Joseph made ready his chariot, and went up to meet Israel his father, and presented himself to him; and he fell on his neck and wept on his neck a good while. And Israel said to Joseph, "Now let me die, for I have seen your face, and know that you are still alive".' (Genesis 46; 29–30). Misericord, Amiens Cathedral; 16th century.

The Exodus from Egypt

The finding of Moses. Exodus 'The Way Out', is one of the Bible's most dramatic books describing the evolution of Jewish religious thought from polytheism to belief in One God who will save mankind, through a leader of unique stature. Thus Moses strides into history. Israel's descendants are now enslaved in Egypt, beset by the tyranny of their masters. To weaken their numbers, the Egyptians have decreed that every male child born to a Hebrew woman must be killed at birth. The child Moses is hidden in the rushes of the river Nile. Pharaoh's daughter finds him there and adopts him as her own. And so a child of the tribe of Levi is brought up at the Egyptian court. To the Egyptians Moses meant 'drawn out of water' but to his own people the name was to symbolize 'the deliverer from bondage' Great Malvern Priory; 15th century.

Above
Moses and the Burning Bush. He has become a shepherd, exiled in Midian, and is grazing his sheep on the slopes of the sacred mountain, Mount Horeb. Suddenly his work is dramatically interrupted as he is brought into the presence of God. Flames leap from the bush, but do not consume it. God tells Moses that he must go back to Egypt to lead his people there from slavery to freedom. In all mythologies fire is a common form in which the deity manifests itself. It is the least substantial of the elements and its flames seem to reach from earth to heaven.

Church of Panagia Phorbiotissa, Asinou, Cyprus; 12th century.

Left
Adoration of the Golden Calf, and the Crossing of the Red Sea. Here Moses is seen, *below,* leading the Israelites out of Egypt and to freedom. At their approach, the seas miraculously fold back, only to close again over the heads of the pursuing Egyptians. To this day Jews celebrate the Passover every spring time, and many levels of its symbolism have been adapted to the Christian faith. Thus the 'matzot' or un-

leavened bread that the Jews eat to remind them of the hurried meal they took on their flight from Egypt has been carried into some Christian communion services where the communicant eats the unleavened wafer. Moses, *left* with the Commandments engraven on stone. If ever the Israelites relapse into the worship of any inferior conception, they bring punishment on themselves. Those, for instance, who conceive of their Creator as a mere fertility God, in this case represented by the golden calf, must die. Chapel of St Philip, Basilica of St Denis, Paris; mid 12th century.

Left and right
The Jews find manna and water. The feast of deliverance from foreign oppression is at an end. The people stumble across the desert once more, in search of the promised land. They are hungry and thirsty, and in their fear of the unknown they turn on Moses. He prays to God, and God sends manna from heaven. In the morning the Israelites find it lying with the dew on the bushes. It is in flakes and tastes like honeycake. Then Moses goes in search of water. He strikes a barren rock with his staff, and water pours from it. The people fill their waterbags, and continue their journey with renewed faith in their God. *Left* Great Malvern Priory, 15th century. *Right* Canterbury Cathedral, 13th century.

Below
The three great foundations of Jewish life were the laws traditionally given through Moses, the Prophets sent and inspired by God to interpret his will, and the writings, consisting of the apparatus of worship – the Psalms, the ritual directions and the annual festivals. God calls Moses to the mountain where he receives the 'Tables of the Law'. God lays down for all time the commandments that are to govern man's behaviour. He must be worshipped as a single being. He discloses to Moses the pillars on which human society must rest: the sacredness of life, the sanctity of marriage, the right to possess property. Here then, we have the dawn of a new awareness in man: the worship of God untainted by magic or grotesque imagery; single, pure, and universal. Moses reads to the people God's commands. Misericord, Gloucester Cathedral.

Top left
Moses and the Golden Calf. While Moses is receiving God's Laws on the mountain, his people grow restless in the valley below. They persuade Aaron to build a golden calf and dance in an orgy of music and ritualistic sacrifice around it. On his return Moses destroys the calf and breaks the Tables of Law as a sign that such people deserve the supreme punishment of losing divine guidance. The symbolic image of the calf here is reminiscent of the Egyptian's worship of Apis and the Canaanites' sacrifice to Baal.

... TI ST EVID RE ISRA(L)(HORATC...

The sacred bull was, above all other animals, connected with fertility. Consciously or unconsciously he was associated with man's sowing of the corn seed, and with the harvest he was to gather from the earth. Church of St. Mary Magdalene, Vezelay, 12th century.

Left
The soothsayer Balaam and his ass. Balek, king of Moab, is afraid of the Israelites advancing on his land. He summons Balaam to lay a curse on them. On his way to the king the soothsayer's ass sees God's angel, and refuses to continue the journey, despite being beaten three times. Eventually the angel becomes visible to Balaam too, who is warned that God's command is greater than the king's. When Balaam sees the Israelite horde encamped on the plain he is filled with prophetic ecstasy and blesses them for all time. All blessings and curses have traditionally been held to carry great power, but Balaam's, as a prophet of God, transcend even these in power. Church of St Andoche, Saulieu, France; 12th century.

Above
The two spies returning from the Promised Land. The Israelites arrive in the wilderness of Paran, midway towards Palestine. Moses sends men to spy out the land. On their return they report that the countryside is rich and green, bringing grapes with them to show the fertility of Canaan. But they warn that the keepers of the land are fierce and warlike giants, the 'sons of Anak'. Here we have the giants of ancient Hebrew mythology, the demi-gods of Genesis. Canterbury Cathedral; 13th century.

The Rise of Israel

Below
The Israelites are living in Palestine, in a constant state of war with the earlier peoples of the land. Tales of heroes and strong men are associated with this as yet unorganized national existence under the judges. Of the strong man Samson, a number of stories are told, although the purpose of some of these is not clear. Here, he seizes the doors of the gates of Gaza and carries them away (Judges 16;3). 17th century German ivory, in the Victoria and Albert Museum, London.

Right
Balaam and his ass and the Tree of Jesse. The importance of Jesse lies solely in the fact that he gave birth to David and through him, in the words of Isaiah, to the Messiah: 'And there shall come forth a rod out of the stem of Jesse, and a branch shall grow out of his roots. And the spirit of the Lord shall rest upon him, the spirit of wisdom and understanding, the spirit of counsel and might, the spirit of knowledge and of the fear of the Lord' (*Isaiah* 2; 1–2). St Zeno, Verona, Italy; 12th century.

Below right
Samson and Delilah. From the time of his birth Samson is marked out by God to accomplish feats of strength and to be the Jew's legendary hero. The secret of his strength lies in his thick hair, which is the outward sign that he is set apart by God. But Delilah entices the secret out of him, and in his sleep she cuts off his hair, letting him fall prey to the Philistines. In India, Mexico and medieval Europe a man's strength was believed to lie in his hair. Canterbury Cathedral; 13th century.

Left
Eli and the prophet Samuel as a boy. Here we have the age-old theme of the childless woman praying to God for a son and offering to sacrifice her most precious possession – i.e. the child – in return for the gift. God answers her prayer and she gives birth to Samuel. When he is two years old she brings him to Eli, the temple priest, to spend the rest of his life in the service of God. Her faith is rewarded again, for Samuel becomes the first prophet of Israel and the anointer of kings. 19th century glass by Burne-Jones, Christ Church Cathedral, Oxford.

Below
David and Goliath. Israel has become a settled nation, but her peace is broken by the Philistines, whose armies threaten to destroy her. As the two armies meet for battle, the Philistine giant, Goliath, challenges one of Israel's men to single combat. The young boy David hears the challenge, pours scorn on Goliath and with neither armour nor sword fells him with a stone from his sling. Goliath was reputedly one of the four descendants of the Rephaim, a tribe of giants who inhabited land on both sides of the Jordan before the coming of the Israelites. Church of St. Mary Magdalene, Vezelay, France; 12th century.

Right
David and the Bear, David and the Lion. 'I have killed lions and bears,' the boy David says to his king, 'and this Philistine will fare no better'. In most parts of the world it has always been considered the height of glory to kill the lion, the king of beasts, and the bear who comes closest to him as a symbol of strength. In this account the beasts are killed by the shepherd to protect his flock. Later, when David is king of Israel, he will deal similarly with his enemies. Winchester Bible; 12th century.

Below
The battle of Mount Gilboa. Saul and his sons were slain here after a period of decline into unpopularity, and David emerged triumphant after a time of civil war, murders and executions which he commemorates in the Lament (2 Samuel 1; 19–27). In the capital F of the first verse of Samuel 2 in the Winchester Bible we see the Amalekite taking the Crown from Saul's head during the closing stages of the battle.

Right
Melchizadek, Abraham with Isaac, Moses, Samuel and David. These figures carved in the 13th century on the central doorway of Chartres Cathedral, France, show the prefigurations of Christ, that is, men who lived long before His day, and whose actions were looked upon as part of the symbolic cycle of events which Christ re-enacted when at last He came. Here are, *left to right*, Melchizadek, with bread and wine, prefiguring the Eu-

charist; Abraham with Isaac bound, prefiguring the cross; Moses holding up one of the tablets; Samuel sacrificing a lamb, prefiguring the sacrifice of Christ; David, into whose tribe Christ was to be born, carrying the instruments of His Passion.

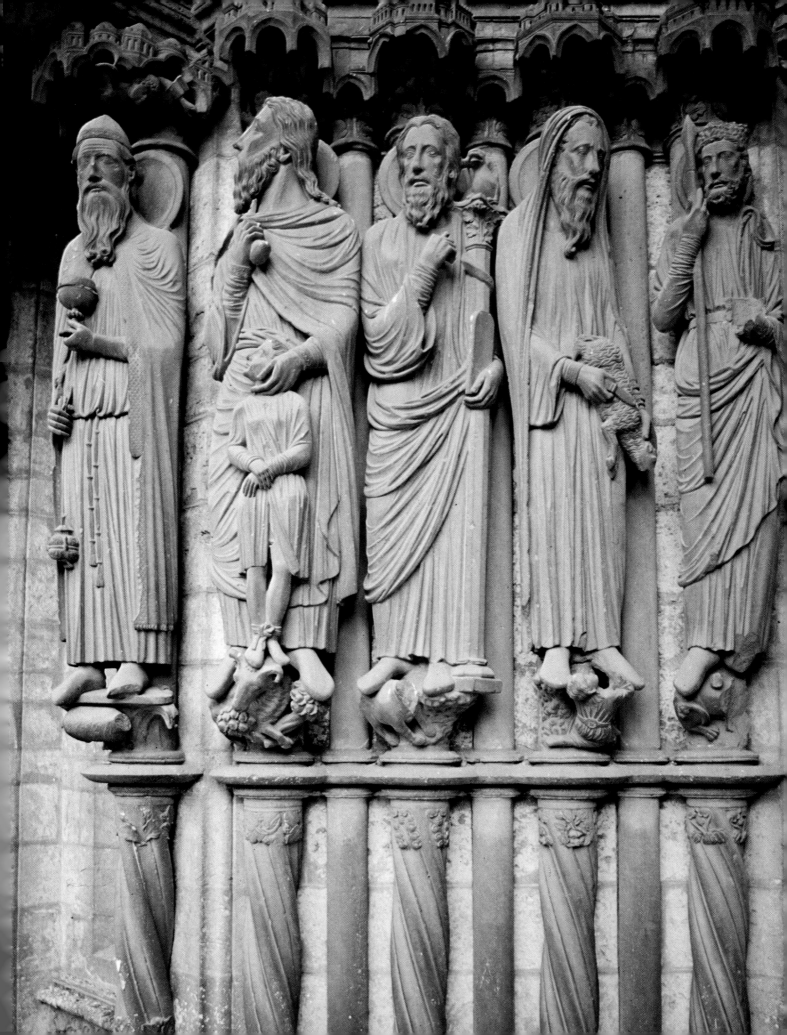

The Prophets

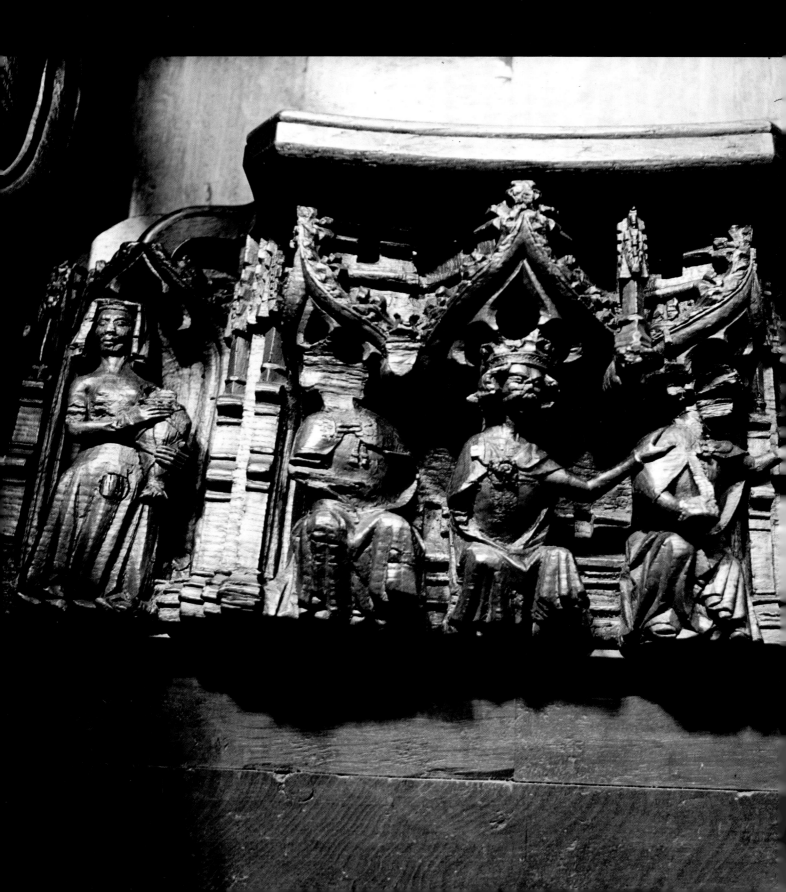

Left
Solomon's Judgment. On the death of King David, his son Solomon already anointed king by Zadok and Nathan takes the throne. In a dream God promises him wisdom. Soon afterwards his wisdom is tested by the rival claims of two women, each with a child. One has died, and each claims that the surviving one is hers. Solomon demands a sword, and orders that the living child be cut in two and half given to each woman. The mother of the living child cries, 'Don't kill him! let her have my child!' Then the king gives judgment that the woman who longs for its life is its true mother. Misericord, Worcester Cathedral; 14th century.

Above
The Visit of the Queen of Sheba. The wisdom of Solomon and the splendour of his court have attracted the Queen of Sheba. She arrives before the king with rich gifts and in turn is overwhelmed by the magnificence of his palace. In Ethiopian Coptic church paintings the queen is traditionally shown receiving every hospitality of the east; she is served dishes so richly spiced that she is finally overcome by a great thirst and goes to the king's well to drink. Solomon meets her there, and the child that is born to them both is mottled black and white, as a token of the mingling of their two races. Canterbury Cathedral; 13th century.

inifrt· postquam mortuus est achab·
Cecidit; ochozias p cancello cenaculi
sui quod habebat in samaria· & egrota
uit· misitq; nuntios dicens ad eos· Ite
consulite beelzebub dm accaron· utru
uiuere queam de infirmitate mea hac
Angelus aute dni locutus est ad helia
thesbiten dicens· Surge ascende in
occursum nuntiorum regis samarie·
& dices ad eos· Numquid non est di
inifrt· ut eatis ad consulendu beelze

Left
Elijah and the messengers of Ahaziah. Many
years have passed since Solomon and Israel's
'Golden Age'. The land has long been
divided into Judah and Israel. Ahab,
Israel's king, whose ivory palace in his new
capital city of Samaria still yields important
fragments to the archaeologist, had died,
but his powerful enemy Elijah the prophet
continues to fight for justice. Elijah meets
messengers from Ahaziah, Israel's new king.
In a powerfully drawn scene in this early
12th century initial in the Winchester Bible,
the strange wild prophet denounces the
king, upon whose frightened messengers fire
is soon to fall from heaven, as the ground
beneath his feet already seems to proclaim.

Above
Elijah in the Chariot of Fire. After Elijah
comes Elisha. Here we see the two great
prophets, with the younger man about to
witness his master's return to God. Suddenly
the sky opens and a chariot drawn by horses
of fire comes down. A whirlwind arises. It
comes between Elijah and Elisha, and lifts
the old man into the chariot and the chariot
into the sky. 'My father, my father!' cries
Elisha, 'The horses and chariots of Israel!'
He picks up the cloak that Elijah had
dropped and puts it over his shoulders. The
spirit of Elijah is in him. Lincoln Cathedral;
19th century.

Right
The Tree of Jesse. This image of an ascending order of generations comes from Isaiah
11; 1–9, where in a marvellously sustained
passage of great lyrical beauty the prophet
foretells the coming of the Messiah. The
symbol of the tree as an embodiment of the
divine spirit is among the oldest and most
widespread of mankind's images. It is the
symbol of vegetation and therefore of life
itself. Window from Chartres Cathedral,
France; 12th century.

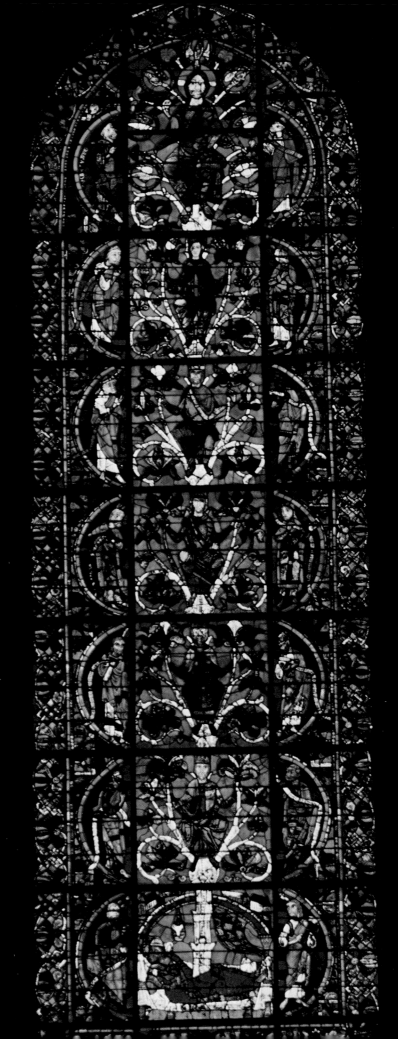

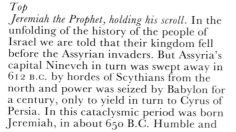

Top
Jeremiah the Prophet, holding his scroll. In the unfolding of the history of the people of Israel we are told that their kingdom fell before the Assyrian invaders. But Assyria's capital Nineveh in turn was swept away in 612 B.C. by hordes of Scythians from the north and power was seized by Babylon for a century, only to yield in turn to Cyrus of Persia. In this cataclysmic period was born Jeremiah, in about 650 B.C. Humble and reluctant to prophesy, he felt compelled by the power of God to call all men to personal repentance and obedience. Supreme poet among the prophets, his sympathy with the bereaved and suffering is expressed with amazing tenderness. San Vitale, Ravenna; 6th century.

Left
The three youths in the fiery furnace. They are to be burnt to death because they have refused to bow to Nebuchadnezzar's golden image. However God protects them and sends an angel to guard them in the flames, and when Nebuchadnezzar's sees them unharmed, he decrees that their God is never to be spoken against. The symbolic custom of death by fire has at different times been widespread among early peoples.

ΔΑΝΙΗΛ

The Druids of Europe, for instance, saw their victims as men possessed of magic and therefore a threat to their survival. Nebuchadnezzar too would have chosen to utterly destroy the power of the Jews by this symbolic burning. Church of Hosios Lukas, Greece; 11th century.

Above
Daniel in the lions' den. Darius becomes king following the fall of Babylon and makes Daniel governor of the land. But Daniel continues to be persecuted by others jealous of his administrative powers. They persuade Darius to decree that anyone who prays to any power but the king's during the next thirty days will be cast into a lions' den. Daniel prays to his God and is cast among the beasts. But the lions do not harm him.

The king, fearing for his safety, visits the pit, finds him unharmed and decrees that he is to be freed. In characteristic Old Testament tradition of retribution the accusers are cast into the pit and the lions devour them, 'bones and all'. Church of Hosios Lukas, Greece; 11th century.

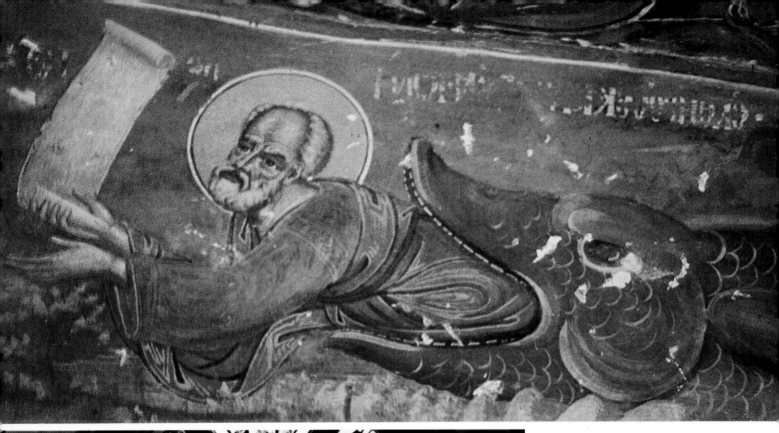

Above
Jonah and the whale. Jonah's importance is not due to his picturesque adventure at sea. God commands him to preach in the heathen city of Nineveh and bring its wicked people to repentance. Instead, he tries to run away from God by sailing to Tarshish. A storm arises and the sailors fear that it is the voice of God in anger. Jonah is blamed for the storm and cast overboard. A fish (not a whale) follows him and later vomits him onto dry land. This became a popular subject in Christian art, especially amongst the 'prefigurings' of the Gospel story, for Christ Himself spoke of Jonah's sojourn in the fish's belly as a sign pointing to His coming sojourn in the tomb. Monastry of Sumela, Trabzon, Turkey; 18th century.

Left
Jonah before Nineveh. God calls Jonah again, and this time he immediately obeys. He goes to Nineveh, Assyria's vast capital – excavations show its walls to have been over 7 miles long – and proclaims its imminent destruction. Its people repent and God defers the disaster. Jonah is angry with God; he wishes to escape and die. He leaves the city and sits at a distance from it in the hot, stony desert. God makes a gourd climb up over him to protect him, but soon a hot wind withers it. Jonah is angry again, and filled with compassion for the plant. Then God tells him that He has pity on *all* men and will forgive them, even though they are not of His chosen race. So Jonah becomes the great herald of God's love for all men. Christ Church Cathedral, Oxford; 17th century.

The Life of Jesus Christ

The Annunciation by the Angel Gabriel to Mary. 'And the angel came to her and said, Hail, thou that art highly favoured, the Lord is with thee: blessed art thou among women. And when she saw him, she was troubled at his saying, and cast in her mind what manner of salutation this should be. And the angel said unto her, Fear not, Mary, for thou hast found favour with God. And, behold, thou shalt conceive in thy womb, and bring forth a son, and shalt call his name JESUS.' (Luke 1:28–31). Thus the mystery begins immediately in our first New Testament picture. The Artist describes Mary, who may have been a girl of Galata, as 'Mother of God'. The model for the angel, who represented 'the other world in terms of this life' could have been a young deacon. Chapel of the Archangel, Galata, Cyprus; 16th century.

Left
Mary goes to a hill town in Judah to see her kinswoman Elizabeth, who is to become the mother of John the Baptist, the last and greatest of the prophets. Elizabeth herself is filled with the spirit of prophecy, 'As soon as your greetings reached my ears, the child within me jumped for joy'. (*Luke* 1;44) Mary bursts into a prophetic song of praise, recalling God's blessings in the past and linking Israel's hope for a Messiah with the promise to Abraham. Freiburg Cathedral, Germany; 14th century.

Above
The life of Mary was a popular subject in medieval art, but little of it can claim to be based on the New Testament. This 13th century ivory figure of the Virgin, which opens like a triptych and is to be found at Evora Cathedral, Portugal, shows (from lowest tier upwards), the Annunciation, the Nativity, the Wise Men, the death of the Virgin, her Assumption to heaven, and her Coronation by her Son. As a young girl she is depicted with long, flowing hair, emblematical of her virginity.

Right
The Journey from Nazareth to Bethlehem. Luke tells us that Joseph and Mary had to return to Bethlehem, Joseph's ancestral home, to take part in a Roman census. The colour blue has traditionally been associated in the west with the mother of Christ. In ecclesiastical symbolism it signifies faith and modesty, humility and expiation. The red of Mary's dress and of Joseph's kirtle here symbolizes divine love and martyrdom, and the green of Joseph's pouch signifies the gladness of the faithful. Notre-Dame-en-Vaux, Chalons-sur-Marne, France; 16th century.

Left
The Annunciation to the Shepherds. 'And there
were in the same country shepherds abiding
in the field, keeping watch over their flock
by night. And, lo, the angel of the Lord
came upon them, and the glory of the Lord
shone round about them: and they were
sore afraid.' (Luke 2: 8–9). Luke tells how
the first to hear of Christ's birth are the
shepherds. He is first accepted by the
humble, and the shepherds also recall
David, His royal ancestor. Cathedral of St
Zeno, Verona, Italy; 11th century.

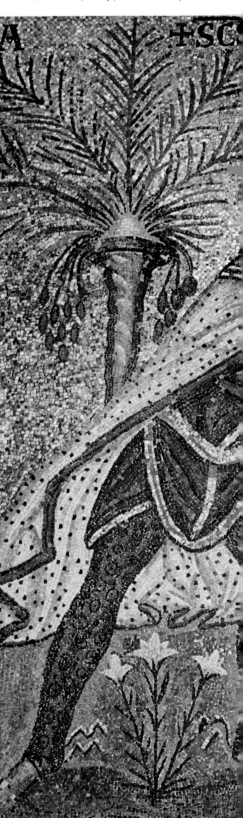

Below left
Angel announcing the birth of Christ to the Shepherds. In the early Church there was some divergence of opinion as to the date of Christ's birth. In the East the date assigned was January 6th and Christmas and Epiphany were celebrated on the same day. In the 4th century the Western date, December 25, was more generally adopted, coinciding as it did with the pagan festival of the birth of the sun on that day. St Peter's, Chauvigny, France; 12th century.

Below and following page
The Adoration of the Magi. The original account in Matthew 2; 1–12 is of wise men following a star which leads them to Bethlehem, where they pay homage to the new-born Christ. *Below* shows a 6th century mosaic from the church of San' Apollinare Nuovo, Ravenna, depicting the event in contemporary style. By the 15th century however, when the stained glass window at Ulm Cathedral, Germany *following page* was painted, the myth around the men had transformed them into three kings, one of

whom was black. The deeper symbolism of the original story nevertheless remains. The gifts they bring are gold, which is a symbol of kings, frank-incense, which is burnt at the altar of God, and myrrh which was used to preserve men's bodies after death. The 'star' referred to by the wise men could possible have been accounted for by the combination of Jupiter and Saturn in 7 B.C.

ALTHASSAR ✛ SCS MELCHIOR ✛ SCS GASPAR

Top right
The dream of the Magi. The wise men's quest for the infant king excites King Herod's jealousy. They are warned in a dream not to return to Herod. Dreams appear in the Bible as vehicles of divine communication, but on a lower level than the visions of prophesy. They usually appear, as here, to those outside the chosen nation, as a means of giving simple advice. This 12th century capital at Autun, France, gives a vigorous presentation of the warning in a dream by an angel – not mentioned in Matthew – pointing to the star while he touches one of the kings, to waken him.

Far right
The Baptism of Christ. 'The next day John seeth Jesus coming unto him, and saith, Behold the Lamb of God, which taketh away the sins of the world. This is he of whom I said, after me cometh a man which is preferred before me: for he was before me' (John 1; 29–30). The sacrament dates back to the early Hebrew custom of ritual washing before an initation. In the New Testament it is taken to represent the moment at which the spirit of God enters a man and he is reborn of that spirit. Church of St Michael and All Angels, Castlefrome, England; 12th century.

Right and following page
The Temptations of Christ. Jesus is baptized by John and withdraws into the wilderness to meditate on His mission and His motives. He is confronted by the devil who challenges Him to prove His supernatural powers. He taunts Jesus to turn the stones of the desert into bread by the use of magic, *right* Church of St Martin, Zillis, Switzerland; 12th century and *over top*, Church of St Antoche, Saulieu, France; 12th century. But to do this would be to use His power for selfish means, and Jesus rejects it. The devil next temps Him to manifest those spectacular signs for which the Jews are waiting *over below* Kariye Camii, Istanbul; 14th century. Jesus rejects this as a false understanding of His power. Finally the devil offers Him both earthly glory and power, but Jesus reminds him of the supreme authority of his Creator and reaffirms God's commandment, 'Thou shalt Worship God, and God alone!'

In Christian art the devil is traditionally depicted black, to symbolize his evil and falsehood. He is more generally represented with a cloven foot, because in Hebrew writings he is called *seirizzim* (goat). The goat became a symbol of uncleaness, and thus was an embodiment of the prince of unclean spirits. The symbolism of the devil with horns, tail and cloven hoofs resembles that of Greek and Roman mythology. In earlier Hebrew mythology however, the symbol of evil was the serpent. In the Book of Job, he is seen as a fallen angel, and later again, in the New Testament, as the spirit of evil. This concept of the dual principles of good and evil is expressed in other cultures, notably in the Persian, where Ormuzd, the creator of all things and judge of the world is in perpetual conflict with Ahriman, the spirit of evil, over whom he will finally triumph.

55

Left and below left
Christ tempted by the devil. See previous page.

Right
The death of John the Baptist. The forerunner of Christ is also killed, his work done. The story is well known, (Mark 6; 14–29) and has ever since made a great impression. The time was not yet ready for the forces of worldliness to be conquered, and John's death heralds the great sacrifice made later by the Son of Man, culminating in the Resurrection. Alabaster, Victoria and Albert Museum London.

Below
The marriage at Cana. Jesus and His mother are invited to a wedding feast. While they are there, the wine runs out and Mary asks her Son to change water into wine. He refuses, saying His time has not come. Later he summons the servants and asks them to fill the waterjars – traditionally used by the Jews for ceremonial cleansing – with fresh water from the well. This water He turns into wine, thus performing His first miracle. The theme of the joyful wedding is later used for Christ Himself who, with His bride the Church on earth, is made one. Church of St Sophia, Trabzon Turkey; 13th century.

Left
The casting out of the Devil, and the harrowing of Hell. A madman is brought to Christ, and is cured of his torment by divine power. Christ summons the evil spirits to come out of the man and take possession of a herd of swine instead. In different times and at different places it has been held that, if the body and spirit of a man are purged of the evil by transferring it to an animal, he can begin a new life, healthy and innocent. Winchester Bible; 12th century.

Below left
Jesus feeding the five thousand. Jesus is surrounded by a great crowd of people and speaks to them of the inner life. He takes five barley loaves and two fish and transforms them by His divine love into enough food to fill the people. John in his account follows his description of this incident with Christ's discourse on Himself as the Bread of Life. He is the true bread which gives life to the world (John 6). Church of St Sophia, Trabzon, Turkey; 13th century.

Top right
Peter walking on the water. The disciples row across the lake from east to west, when a great storm arises and they lose their bearings. All is darkness around them, until a figure of light comes towards them. It is Jesus, walking on the water. He calls to them to have no fear and the storm is followed by calm and safe arrival at the shore. The sign here is that the presence of Jesus puts an immediate end to danger and conflict. Peter, always the most impulsive of the disciples, jumps from the ship and walks towards Him. The artist here shows him suddenly realizing what he is doing; his faith in his master vanishes, and he begins to sink, until he is rescued by Jesus. St Peter Mancroft, Norwich, England, 15th century.

Far right
The Raising of Lazarus. Jesus is called to the sickbed of his friend Lazarus; by the time He gets there Lazarus is already dead. Jesus is led to his burial place, where he cries with a loud voice, 'Lazarus, come forth. And he that was dead came forth, bound hand and foot, with gravecloths; and his face was bound about with a napkin. Jesus said unto them, Loose him, and let him go.' (John 11; 25–44) Sarcophagus in San Vitale, Ravenna, Italy; 7th century.

Right
The Transfiguration. Jesus selects His three closest disciples, Peter, James and John, to accompany Him up the Mount of Transfiguration. There they see Him, transfigured, at some distance to themselves, with Moses on one side and Elijah on the other as the representatives of the Law and the Prophets which find their fulfilment in Christ. It is Jesus who now offers men a moral choice; to follow Him means a return, beyond the confines of time and history, to God Himself. Church of Daphni Monastry, Greece; 11th century.

Jesus Christ
and the Church

Below left
The Entry into Jerusalem (top row); Judas receives 30 pieces of silver; last supper (2nd row); the betrayal in the garden of Gethsemane. (bottom row). Jesus fulfils His role as predicted by the prophets of the Old Testament; He enters Jerusalem 'meek and riding upon an ass', and is hailed as the son of David by the people. He is given the chance to escape; He refuses, and lets the purpose that God the Father has ordained for Him and for the salvation of all mankind, be worked out through him. St Martin's Zillis, Switzerland; 12th century.

Below
The Last Supper. 'And as they did eat, Jesus took bread, and blessed and brake it, and gave to them and said, Take, eat. This is my body. And he took the cup, and when he had given thanks, he gave it to them: and they all drank of it. And he said unto them, This is my blood of the new testament, which is shed for many' (Mk 14, 22–24). 'Jesus said, A new commandment I give to you, that you love one another, as I have loved you ... Greater love has no man than this, that a man lay down his life for his friends. You are my friends' (John 13; 11–15; 14). Around this scene was to grow the fable of the holy grail, that cup which Jesus held, and whose quest was to become the subject of medieval legend, romance and allegory. In the Renaissance banquet scene, Judas is still present, and Jesus has caused consternation by speaking of the traitor in their midst. Church of Notre Dame, Chalons-sur-Marne, France; 16th century. The 13th century glass *bottom* portrays the moment after the bread has been broken, when the Cup is being passed round; Bourges Cathedral, France; 13th century.

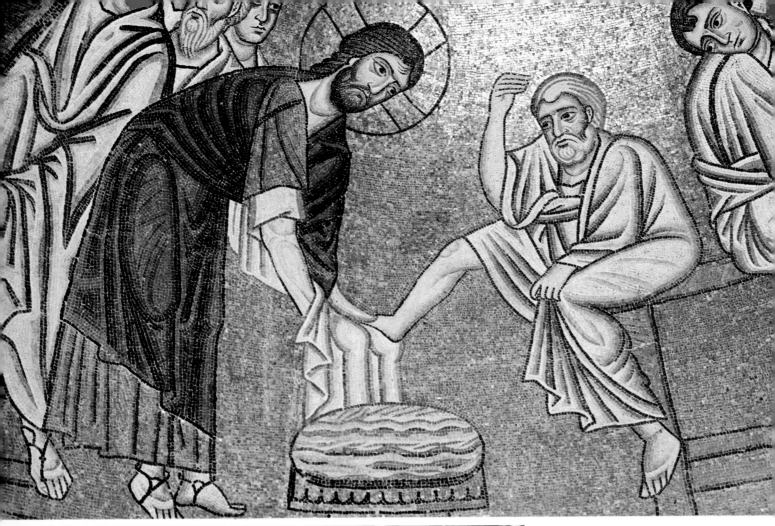

Above
Christ washing the Disciples' Feet. 'And he poured water into a basin, and began to wash the disciples' feet, and to wipe them with the towel wherewith he was girded' (John 13; 5) The Fourth Gospel reports at length the final discourses between Jesus and His followers before their departure to Gethsemane. First and most important, Jesus leaves them a demonstration of the Christian view of greatness – it must imply humility, and be expressed in service. The higher the position, the humbler the service. So Jesus assumes the role of the humblest slave, who washes the guests' feet. Peter, seen here in a superb mosaic, cannot endure it, and points to his head as needing cleansing. Hosios Lukas, Greece; 11th century.

Left
The Agony in the Garden. Jesus takes his closest friends, Peter, James and John to watch with Him in the Garden of Gethsemane through the dead hour before dawn. 'He said to them, My soul is exceedingly sorrowful unto death: tarry ye here, and watch. And he went forward a little, and fell on the ground, and prayed that, if it were possible, the hour might pass from him (Mk 14; 33–35), but the hour does not pass, nor the cup that He must drink before His mortal agony is lifted.' Ulm Cathedral, stained glass by Hans Acker; 15th century.

Right
The Crucifixion and the Pieta. 'And when they were come to the place, which is called Calvary, there they crucified him, and the malefactors, one on the right hand, and the other on the left.' *continued overleaf*

Continued from previous page
'Then said Jesus, Father, forgive them; for
they know not what they do' (Luke 23;
33–34). The cross is not exclusively a
Christian symbol. Early Norsemen erected
runic crosses over the graves of kings and
heroes, while the Egyptians and the Aztecs
among others used it as a sacred symbol.
Notre Dame, Chalons-sur-Marne, France;
16th century.

Above
The empty tomb. As soon as possible after the
Sabbath, 'Early on the Sunday morning
while it was still dark' (John 20), Mary
Magdalene went to the tomb and found it
empty. The four Gospels differ as to what
happened, but this is natural. Closely
similar descriptions from different people
would be suspect. They had seen Jesus die.
That, for them, was until Easter morning,
the end. The events of that morning were
outside their experience, their means of
expression, since they were divine, other

worldly events. Panagia Phorbiotissa
Church Asinou, Nikitari. Cyprus; 14th
century.

Opposite
The Resurrection and Anastasis. Three
different human conceptions of what the
Resurrection of Christ may have been like,
from the literal rendering from Freiburg
right, to the primordial image from Southfleet England, *top right*, and ending with
the spiritual vision from Istanbul *top left*.
The Western artists have portrayed the
scene in local terms, so there is a coffin
rather than a cave, and in the garden (left-
hand scene) Jesus even holds a spade (John
20; 15–17). The painting from Istanbul
shows Christ striding above the gates of Hell
and above Satan and raising up Adam and
Eve, John the Baptist and David from the
dead. For man, the deepest quest has
always been his relationship with the
infinite, and it is here that Christ's death
and resurrection take on their greatest

significance. The Bible relates how the long
fall from God's grace, which began with
Adam and Eve, ends with Christ's sacrifice;
man may now return to God from whom he
came. By a complex system of symbolism
and mythology the early Hebrew writers
had seen the splintering of human consciousness as beginning with the fall of Adam.
In the New Testament man's wholeness is
restored through Christ. Before Christ, he
was a creature in whom both the limited
and the eternal co-existed; for by eating of
the tree of the knowledge of good and evil
he became a prisoner of the physical world.
But God came to earth to free man, extending his consciousness through Jesus Christ
as light extends through darkness. At last
the duality in man is healed; his sin is
forgiven and he has his spiritual transcend-
ency restored to him through Christ. Freiburg Cathedral, Germany; 15th century.
Church of St. Nicholas, Southfleet, England;
15th century. Kariye Camii. Istanbul; 14th
century.

Left
The Ascension Portal, Chartres Cathedral, France; 12th century. 'And when he had spoken these things, while they beheld, he was taken up; and a cloud received him out of their sight' (Acts 1; 9–10). The angels carved here in stone represent the presence of God, while the figures that surround Jesus are largely allegorical. From the first centuries after Christ's death until the end of the Middle Ages a physical confrontation with an angel was seen as something that happened to many people, good or bad, in their lifetime. These encounters were the subject of innumerable folktales, some of which were inspired by an earlier, pagan mythology.

Below
Pentecost. 'And suddenly there came a sound from heaven as of a rushing mighty wind, and it filled all the house where they were sitting. And there appeared unto them cloven tongues like as of fire, and it sat upon each of them. And they were all filled with the Holy Ghost, and began to speak with other tongues, as the spirit gave them utterance' (Acts 2; 1–4) The symbolism of wind and fire makes the understanding of the Holy Spirit easier. The time of this happening was at the feast of Pentecost, when Jews give thanks for the wheat harvest and for the giving of the Law to Moses. The festival is also known as Whitesunday. Hosios Lokas, Greece; 11th century.

Right and below
The Last Judgment. 'When the Son of man shall come in his glory, and all the holy angels with him, then shall he sit upon the throne of his glory. And before him shall be gathered all nations: and he shall separate them one from another, as a shepherd divideth his sheep from the goats ... Then shall the king say to them on his right hand, Come ye blessed of my Father, inherit the kingdom prepared for you from the foundation of the world: For when I was an hungered, ye gave me meat: I was thirsty, and ye gave me drink: I was a stranger, and ye took me in: Naked, and ye clothed me: I was sick, and ye visited me: I was in prison, and ye came unto me. Then shall the righteous answer him, saying, Lord, when saw we thee an hungered, and fed thee? or thirsty, and gave thee drink? ... and the king shall answer and say unto them, Truly I say unto you, in as much as you have done it unto one of the least of these my brethren, you have done it unto me!' (Mathew 25; 31 ;40). This must be one of the most frequently portrayed subjects in Christian Churches. The 13th century carvings on the West doors of Notre Dame in Paris show typical scenes, as does the 16th century west window at Fairford church, Glos., England *right*; the dead rising from Hell at the sound of the Last Trumpet, the scales of judgement, and behind Christ sit the Virgin and Apostles.

The Future

Below (see also previous page)
The Last Judgment. Top, centre, St Michael weighing the souls of the risen dead; *left* and *right*, saints praying for the dead. *Middle row, left*, an angel carries souls in a sheet to judgment; *centre*, an angel leads some to heaven, while a demon leads others to hell. *Right*, demons thrust the souls of the damned into the mouth of a monster representing hell. *Bottom left, centre* and *right*, angels blowing the last trump. Both Christians and Jews have in time of persecution found comfort in Hebrew apocalyptic writers, applying their visions to a threatened world. Bourges Cathedral; France; 13th century.

Right
The Son of Man. The observations of modern thinkers such as Jung have thrown a new light on man's need to relate the abstract image of God to the centre of his being. To Jung, the symmetrical arrangement of the circle and the square represent the centre of the personality, the instrument of contemplation. This conjunction was frequently portrayed in the Christian art of the Middle Ages, as in Bourges Cathedral, France; 13th century. Christ is shown here as the central point of a figuration that recalls the pattern of a flower, cross or wheel – the *mandela* of man's being.

Below Right
Sarcophagus of the twelve Apostles. Church of San Apollinare in Classe, Ravenna; 6th century. Christ chose and trained twelve men to preach His message and continue His work of physical, emotional and spiritual healing. They were to 'carry neither purse nor script, nor shoes, and salute no man by the way' (Luke 10; 4). 'If any man would come after me, let him deny himself and take up his cross and follow me' (Mark 8; 34). Innumerable folk tales were later to grow out of the actions of the apostles and disciples, reaching their climax with the veneration of relics in the Middle Ages

Following page top
St Paul and St Peter. The two great pillars of the Church, symbolized respectively by a scroll denoting the new law brought to the Gentiles and cross-keys, the insignia of the Pope who acts as Christ's representative on earth. In the mosaic from the Church of Santa Maria, Cosmedin, Ravenna; 5th century, they are depicted standing either side of an empty throne, reminiscent of the pre-Hellenic custom of setting up empty thrones on which the gods, invisible to human eyes, may sit.
Below left is a detail of *St Peter*. Here we see more clearly the 'keys to the kingdom of heaven' which Christ left in his keeping. Tradition has it that he was crucified in A.D. 65 with his head downwards, prefering to die like this since, as he said, he was not worthy to suffer the same death as his Master. The location of his remains under the high altar of St Peter's, Rome, was announced as recently as 1950, and their authenticity was confirmed by the Pope in 1968.

Above
The Conversion of St Paul. The personality
and preaching of Paul has influenced the
Christian Church more than that of any
other apostle. He was on his way to Damas-
cus 'breathing out threatenings and slaugh-
ter against the disciples' (Acts 9;1) when
suddenly he was blinded by a shaft of light
from heaven and heard Jesus's voice. For
three days Saul lived in darkness, until his
sight was restored by the laying on of hands
by Ananias and he was baptized as a
Christian. From then on he became the
Church's most indefatigable and eloquent
exponent. Lincoln Cathedral; 19th century.

Below left
Apostles fishing. 'Simon Peter said to them, I
will go fishing. They said to him, We will
go with thee. They went forth, and entered
into a ship immediately, and they caught
nothing'. But Jesus calls to them from the
shore, 'Cast the net on the right side of the
ship, and you shall find. They cast therefore,
and now they were not able to draw it for
the multitude of fishes' (John 21; 3–6). In
Hebrew and Western mythology the fish
has traditionally represented the soul of
man; it was adopted by the early Christians
as the symbol for Christ's Church and for
Christ Himself. (The Greek word for fish-
ICTHUS- was a mnemonic for Jesus Christ,
son of God, Saviour.) St Martin's church,
Zillis, Switzerland; 12th century.

Above
The Apocalypse. The final confrontation of
the powers of good and evil occupies an
important place in mythologies. It is
symbolically described in the Book of
Revelation as a time of great suffering and
chaos in which the forces of evil are finally
conquered and all creation is made one
with God. Thus the numerous visions in
Revelation are intended to comfort those
who try to live the Christian life amidst
adversity, for to the patient there will come
peace and light in the end. The key to
much of the symbolism is lost, though it has
been suggested that the number three
means heaven, four means the earth, and
the number seven is the blending of the two.
The great East window, York Minster,
England; 15th century.

interpretations are inspired by the animal kingdom, since the apocalyptic writers could not convey the presence of evil except as an aberration of the physical world. The 'powers of darkness' and the 'principalities' of St Paul belong to an altogether more abstract, Hellenistic tradition. *Below right* we see the Prostitution of the Beast, standing for the Roman Empire that so supressed the Jews, and the whole of Babylon embodying the luxury, vice, splendour and tyranny that was the enemy of the early Church. *Overleaf.* Finally we come to where the Angel shows John the River of Paradise. 'And he showed me a pure river of water of life, clear as crystal, proceeding out of the throne of God and of the Lamb. In the midst of the stream of it, and on either side of the river, was the tree of life, which bare twelve manner of fruits, and yielded her fruit every month: and the leaves of the tree were for the healing of the nations. And there shall be no more curse: but the throne of God and of the Lamb shall be in it; and his servants shall serve him: 'And they shall see his face; and his name shall be in their foreheads. And there shall be no night there; and they need no candle, neither light of the sun; for the Lord God giveth them light: and they shall reign for ever and ever ... I am Alpha and Omega, the beginning and the end, the first and the last.' (Revelation. 22; 1–5 13.).

Above
'And there was war in heaven: Michael and his angels fought against the dragon ... And the dragon prevailed not, neither was his place found any more in heaven. And the great dragon was cast out ... Satan, the Devil, was cast out into the earth' (Revelation. 12; 7–9). This theme of spiritual rebellion which finds its counterpart in Mohammedan myth, runs through much of the literature of the Bible. Here, as in the Mohammedan sagas, Satan does not repent; the forces of good and of evil are irreconcilable. Norwich Cathedral; 14th century.

These pages and overleaf
The end of time is the theme that runs through the four scenes above. They are inspired by the *visions of St John the Divine in the Book of Revelation*, and are taken from a series of tapestries at Angers, France, dating from the 14th century. *Below* we see the Second Angel blowing his trumpet, at which mountains of fire are cast into the sea and turn it to blood. *Top right* shows the Sixth Angel emptying the bowl of God's anger on the earth as a prelude to the great battle between the forces of good and evil at Armageddon. The devils, dragons and monsters that figure in these and similar

Bibliography

Acknowledgments

Short Book List

The Lion Handbook to the Bible, Lion Publishing, 1973

Anderson, MD,	*The Imagery of British Churches*, Murray, 1955
Black, M,	*Peake's Commentary on the Bible*, Nelson, 1962
Blunt, AWF,	*Israel, Social & Religious Development*, OUP, 1924
Bovini, G,	*Sans Vitale di Ravenna*, "Silvana" Editoriale d'arte, Milan, 1955
Bultmann, R,	*Jesus Christ and Mythology* SCM, 1960
Demus, O,	*Byzantine Mosaic Decoration*, Kegan Paul, 1947
Eliade, M,	*Myths, Dreams and Mysteries*, Harvill, 1960
Hamilton, JA,	*Byzantine Architecture and Decoration*, Batsford, 1933
Harrison, F,	*The Painted Glass of York*, SPCK, 1927
Henry, F,	*Irish Art during the Viking Invasions*, Methuen, 1967
Macquarrie, J,	*An Existentialist Theology*, SCM, 1955
	The Scope of Demythologising, SCM 1960
Malavez, L,	*The Christian Message and Myth*, SCM, 1958
Richardson, A,	*Dictionary of Christian Theology*, SCM, 1969
	A Theological Word Book of the Bible, SCM, 1954
Robertson, A,	*Bible of St Mark, Venice*, Allen, 1898

Biblical quotations are mainly from the *New English Bible*, OUP, CUP, 1961

The publishers would like to thank the following for their kind permission to photograph subjects for this book:

The Dean & Chapter of Salisbury Cathedral.
The Dean & Chapter of Worcester Cathedral.
The Dean & Chapter of Winchester Cathedral.
The Dean & Chapter of Wells Cathedral.
The Dean & Chapter of Christ Church Oxford.
The Dean & Chapter of Lincoln Cathedral.
The Dean & Chapter of Norwich Cathedral.
The Dean & Chapter of Canterbury Cathedral.
The Dean & Chapter of Gloucester Cathedral.
The Victoria & Albert Museum. Chartres Cathedral. Monsieur Paganelli, Monuments Historiques, Tours. Soprintendenza ai Monumenti, Ravenna. Dekan, Ulmer Münster, Ulm. Dekan, Freiburger Münster, Freiburg. Monuments Historiques de Paris, St. Denis, Angers, Autun, Amiens, Bourges. Mons. Le Curé de Notre Dame, Chalons-Sur-Marne. The Vicar of Malvern.

The Vicar of Malvern.

Page 17 top left, 49 top and 50 bottom, photographs by F.H.C. Birch, Sonia Halliday Photographs. Contents page: The flight into Egypt Bellieu Church, Bulgaria.

Sonia Halliday & Laura Lushington would like to thank Martine Klotz of Paris, and Dietmar Lüdke of Freiburg for their valuable help in obtaining permission for them to photograph in France and Germany.